4th Watch Books™

Forward

Our purpose for publishing the documents issued by the National Institute of Standards and Technology (NIST) is twofold. First of all, each NIST title in and of itself is very informative, however I am of the opinion that they should be looked at from the standpoint that each title is an integral part of a holistic cybersecurity strategy. Rather than look at each title just by itself, we need to look at them in groups based on how they are interrelated and designed to work together to improve cybersecurity.

For example, this particular group on Authentication/Identity security includes the following titles:

NIST SP 800-63-3	Digital Identity Guidelines
NIST SP 800-63a	Digital Identity Guidelines - Enrollment and Identity Proofing
NIST SP 800-63b	Digital Identity Guidelines - Authentication and Lifecycle Management
NIST SP 800-63c	Digital Identity Guidelines - Federation and Assertions
NIST SP 800-178	Comparison of Attribute Based Access Control (ABAC) Standards for Data Service Applications
NISTIR 7924	Reference Certificate Policy
NISTIR 8112	Attribute Metadata - Draft

In order to assemble the entire picture of authentication/identity security – from what it is, how it works, what the vulnerabilities are and how to mitigate them, one must examine all of these documents. Only by going through all of them can a person understand the complete picture. Leave one of them out and you would be missing a valuable piece of the authentication/identity security puzzle.

Why buy a book you can download for free?

That brings me to the second reason to publish the NIST standards and that is the logistics of it all. These 7 publications consist of 771 pages. That's enough paper to fill two large three-ring binders. Nobody has a secretary anymore, so an engineer that is paid $75 an hour has to do this. The amount of time it would take an engineer to print all 7 publications (using a network printer shared with 100 other people – and it's out of paper, and the toner is low), punch holes in 771 pages and assemble the binders would easily take half a day.

Our ability to deliver any NIST document quickly and efficiently is unmatched because we are printing books on demand using Createspace (an Amazon.com company), so the titles are easy to find and simple to order. Just search Amazon.com by NIST number or tile and you can have a copy shipped to you in a matter of days. We print all books a full 8 ½ inches by 11 inches, with large text. If there are color images in the publication, the book is probably in color, unless the color is merely decorative, in which case we print in black and white to keep the cost to you as low as possible.

Luis Ayala,

My email is cybah@webplus.net   Our website is: cybah.webplus.net

4th Watch Books is a Service Disabled Veteran Owned Small Business (SDVOSB).

Following is an excerpt from the book titled "**Cyber-Physical Attack Defenses: Preventing Damage to Buildings and Utilities**", by Luis Ayala (available at Amazon.com, Barnes & Noble and Books-a-Million).

Hacking into Building Controls Systems (BCS), Industrial Controls Systems (ICS), and Supervisory Controls and Data Acquisition (SCADA) networks is not the same as breaking into enterprise networks that process information. BCS, ICS and SCADA systems are much more complex. Breaking into a controls system is only a means to an end. The target is not the network itself, it is the equipment being controlled.

Cyber-physical attacks represent the weaponization of the Internet

Although designing a catastrophic cyber-physical attack scenario to exploit a particular physical process requires a solid engineering background and in-depth destructive knowledge of the target controls system (Cyber-Physical Attack Engineering) – you don't need an engineering background to figure out how to turn equipment off.

In addition, a typical ICS contains multiple control loops and sometimes the control loops are nested and/or cascading, so the set point for one loop is based on the process variable output from another loop. Interrupting one process can have a ripple effect through the factory. Supervisory control loops and lower-level loops operate continuously over the duration of a process with cycle times of milliseconds.

A cracker doesn't need to have an engineering degree to figure out that a large change in the setpoint (or process values) on a proportional feedback system will have a larger effect than a small change that would be tolerated based on the sensitivity of the control system and the process. But, even a small change that results in sluggish response in the short-term could have a major effect over a relatively long period of time.

The only saving grace is that a newbie or script kiddie will not thoroughly understand complex manufacturing processes. While a newbie may be able to turn off the lights in the factory, I doubt he would know how to increase the deadband (an interval of a signal domain where no action occurs - the system is 'dead' - i.e. the output is zero) on voltage regulators, or cause repeated activation-deactivation cycles.

Hacking a chemical plant to create a weapon of mass destruction (a Bhopal-style catastrophic failure) for example, requires knowledge of physics, chemistry and engineering, as well as a great deal about how the network is laid out, and a keen understanding of process-aware defensive systems. The most a newbie could hope to do is to turn something off.

A well-qualified attacker (such as a foreign security service) hitting a building or utilities controls network seeks to take control over the equipment. Those crackers understand the equipment they will be controlling. No offense but, most IT guys are not familiar with electrical and mechanical equipment, industrial and manufacturing equipment, or utility equipment, so they wouldn't know how to defend them. That's because they don't know the equipment or processes being controlled.

The same is true of the folks in charge of physical security at these facilities. The typical security guys don't know anything about electrical and mechanical systems, or how computer networks are designed. Let's face it, they don't have the budget or the training to deal with these new threats.

The owner is looking to the facility guys, the IT guys and the security guys to work together to defend their physical plant, and in many cases, these guys aren't even talking to each other. Most of the time, they think cyber-physical security is someone else's responsibility! In essence, "nobody is minding the store". An effective defense against cyber-physical attacks requires procedural safeguards, such as frequent password changes, equipment inspections, random drills, security awareness programs, records retention programs, etc.

So, what is the big deal?

On December 3 1984, in Bhopal, India there was an industrial accident at a pesticide plant that immediately killed at least 3,800 people and caused significant morbidity and premature death for many thousands more. That was only one incident with a release of only 40 tons of methyl isocyanate gas. Of course, this was an accident and not a cyber-physical attack, but it should give you an idea what could happen in a worst-case scenario.

Another example is what actually happened at a Chrysler assembly plant. An attacker shut down one auto plant with a worm that quickly spread to all other Chrysler plants, idling 50,000 workers. These were professionally-installed industrial control networks with firewalls and safety features. I suspect they were protected in much the same way that many enterprise networks are protected today.

The bad news is that crackers are getting better at what they do. In the good old days, an attacker would use a virus or worm to take over your computer. Nowadays, they can attack your computer without loading any files at all. That's because all the files they need to take control are already loaded on your computer. That's called a Fileless Cyber-Attack. All they need to do is trick you into giving them permission to access those files. Anti-virus software has gotten very good at detecting and stopping a computer virus. Attackers find it much easier to fool a human using social engineering.

In order for you to begin to understand what is going through the mind of someone trying to break into your computer network, I include a lot of Hackerspeak, or Leet-speak in this book. See the definitions a little further on. This should give you some insight into the mind of a hacker.

This book was written to help Owners, Architects, Engineers, and facilities and infrastructure maintenance personnel understand the vulnerability of SCADA systems, building controls systems, and industrial controls systems to cyber-physical attack. The book includes simple descriptions of the vulnerabilities (attack vectors) of automated equipment controls common to buildings, industry and utilities. The book also lists the different types of cyber-physical attacks discovered. It is a handy desk reference for Architects, Engineers, Building Managers, Students, Researchers and Consultants interested in preventing cyber-physical attacks. Remember, a "hacker" and a "cracker" are two different meanings so please stop referring to hackers as bad guys.

The price of connectivity is less security. The more connected a device is, the less secure it will be.

7. Monitor the Process Equipment Looking for Anomalies

It is probably easier to detect a cyber-physical attack (when it occurs) by looking at how the equipment is operating than it is to detect subtle software anomalies or dropped packets. Although boiler water temperature and pressure rising dangerous levels doesn't necessarily signal that a cyber-physical attack is underway, it could be an attack. Don't assume it isn't a cyber-attack out of hand. Look for signs that the controls have been manipulated. Compare what the computer says is happening with what the equipment is actually doing. Remember, a sneaky attacker will change the setpoints higher than normal so the computer will not know something is wrong.

Malicious attackers are more likely to use the process control systems to make equipment "misbehave" while appearing to operate normally. At the Iranian nuclear plant, Stuxnet manipulated the calibration systems so the plant workers didn't see the real pressure readings that would have flagged the problems with the devices early on. Had the workers manually checked the equipment itself frequently, they would have noticed the discrepancy.

A malicious attacker would schedule his attack when it would be less likely to be detected or when it could do the most damage. Startup and shutdown of a process plant are the two most dangerous operational modes of the plant. A well-qualified attacker would know the planned startup sequence of operations and manipulate the amount of heat or the flow of chemicals to corrupt the process and damage the hardware.

For example, industrial distillation is typically performed in large, vertical cylindrical columns known as distillation towers or distillation columns. The amount of heat entering a distillation column is a crucial operating parameter, addition of excess or insufficient heat to the column can lead to foaming, weeping, entrainment, or flooding. If the column contains liquid during pressuring, excessive vapor flows will cause flooding and gas lifting of the liquid, resulting in liquid discharge into relief header and damage the column internals.

The information in this NIST title directly addresses the concerns I articulated in my Cyber-Physical Attack Defenses book. By implementing the attached standard, hopefully your system can survive an attempted cyber-physical attack.

Luis Ayala

Second Draft NISTIR 7924

Reference Certificate Policy

Harold Booth
Andrew Regenscheid

National Institute of
Standards and Technology
U.S. Department of Commerce

Second Draft NISTIR 7924

Reference Certificate Policy

Harold Booth
Andrew Regenscheid
Computer Security Division
Information Technology Laboratory

May 2014

U.S. Department of Commerce
Penny Pritzker, Secretary

National Institute of Standards and Technology
Patrick D. Gallagher, Under Secretary of Commerce for Standards and Technology and Director

National Institute of Standards and Technology Interagency or Internal Report 7924
95 pages (May 2014)

Public comment period: *May 29, 2014* through *August 1, 2014*

National Institute of Standards and Technology

Attn: Computer Security Division, Information Technology Laboratory

100 Bureau Drive (Mail Stop 8930) Gaithersburg, MD 20899-8930

nistir7924-comments@nist.gov

Reports on Computer Systems Technology

The Information Technology Laboratory (ITL) at the National Institute of Standards and Technology (NIST) promotes the U.S. economy and public welfare by providing technical leadership for the Nation's measurement and standards infrastructure. ITL develops tests, test methods, reference data, proof of concept implementations, and technical analyses to advance the development and productive use of information technology. ITL's responsibilities include the development of management, administrative, technical, and physical standards and guidelines for the cost-effective security and privacy of other than national security-related information in Federal information systems.

Abstract

The purpose of this document is to identify a baseline set of security controls and practices to support the secure issuance of certificates. This baseline was developed with publicly-trusted Certification Authorities (CAs) in mind. These CAs, who issue the certificates used to secure websites using TLS and verify the authenticity of software, play a particularly important role online. This document formatted as a Reference Certificate Policy (CP). We expect different applications and relying party communities will tailor this document based on their specific needs. It was structured and developed so that the CP developer can fill in sections specific to organizational needs and quickly produce a suitable CP. This Reference CP is consistent with the Internet Engineering Task Force (IETF) Public Key Infrastructure X.509 (IETF PKIX) Certificate Policy and Certification Practices Framework.

Keywords

certification authority; certificate authority certificate policy; digital certificate; public key infrastructure

Acknowledgments

This publication was developed in collaboration with the National Security Agency (NSA). The Federal Information Security Management Act of 2002 mandates that NIST consult with the NSA on standards and guidelines for securing information systems. In particular, NIST wishes to acknowledge the substantial contributions made by Mike Boyle, Deb Cooley, and Mike Jenkins of the NSA, along with NSA contractor Jeffrey Burke of National Security Partners, who served on this publication's development team. These individuals helped to develop the technical content of these guidelines, provided editorial review, and assisted in the adjudication of public comments.

The authors wish to thank their colleagues who reviewed drafts of this document and contributed to its technical content. In particular, the authors appreciate the contributions of the Federal PKI's Certificate Policy Working Group, whose "X.509 Certificate Policy For The U.S. Federal PKI Common Policy Framework" document was the basis for many sections in this document.

Table of Contents

List of Appendices

Foreword

Background

Certification Authorities (CAs), and the infrastructure they support, form the basis for one of the primary mechanisms for providing strong assurance of identity in online transactions. The widely placed trust in CAs is at the heart of security mechanisms used to protect business and financial transactions online. Notably, protocols such as Transport Layer Security (TLS) rely on CAs to identify servers and clients in web transactions. Governments around the world rely on CAs to identify parties involved in transactions with them.

However, recent high-profile security breaches at major CAs trusted by widely used operating systems and browsers have highlighted both the critical role CAs play in securing electronic transactions, as well as the need to strongly protect them from malicious attacks. Analyses have revealed that these security breaches were often the result of insufficient security controls being in place on the computer systems and networks at these CAs, and sometimes exacerbated by weak record keeping. Third-party auditing programs, whose role was to verify that proper security controls were in place, were not sufficient to identify these lapses in security.

The purpose of this document is to provide security guidance on a baseline set of security controls and practices to support the secure issuance of certificates. In particular, the baseline has been developed with publicly-trusted CAs in mind, providing an appropriate level of assurance to support typical commercial and non-national security government systems and applications, i.e., a moderate assurance level. These CAs, who issue the certificates used to secure websites using TLS and verify the authenticity of software, play a particularly important role online.

Reference Certificate Policy

This baseline set of controls has been written in the form of a "certificate policy." As defined by ITU Recommendation X.509, a "certificate policy" is "a named set of rules that indicates the applicability of a certificate to a particular community and/or class of application with common security requirements." That is, a certificate policy, or CP, defines the expectations and requirements of the relying party community that will trust the certificates issued by its CAs. The governance structure that represents the relying party is known as the Policy Authority. The Policy Authority is responsible for identifying the appropriate set of requirements for a given community, and oversees the CAs that issue certificates for that community.

In particular, this document was developed as a reference certificate policy. We expect different applications and relying party communities will tailor this document based on their specific needs. It was structured and developed so that the CP developer can fill in sections specific to organizational needs and quickly produce a suitable CP. This Reference CP is consistent with the Internet Engineering Task Force (IETF) Public Key Infrastructure X.509 (IETF PKIX) Certificate Policy and Certification Practices Framework [RFC3647].

The United States Government's Federal PKI Common Policy was used as a base document for this reference certificate policy. The FPKI Common Policy is widely recognized for clearly articulating the requirements for certificate issuance for the certificates covered by this set of policies, which are primarily used by government entities to authenticate to government systems. Within this reference certificate policy, we've adapted the US Government's requirements to be more appropriate to the wider PKI community. We also significantly updated the requirements in the computer, lifecycle and network security control sections.

Originally conceived of as primarily offline systems, the architecture of large, modern CAs has increasingly moved online. Registration Authorities (RAs), the part of the CA infrastructure that validates identities of subscribers, communicate with subscribers and CAs over the Internet, and CAs frequently issue certificates, based on the identity-proofing by RAs, through automated processes. This change in architecture, along with the changing threat environment faced by online systems, necessitates additional security mechanisms in place at CAs. The CA community has long recognized the need for tight physical security and key management at CAs, but these security controls must also be accompanied by computer, lifecycle and network security controls of appropriate strength.

Using this Document

This document is designed to be used as a template and guide for writing a CP for a specific community or a Certification Practice Statement (CPS) for a specific CA. The controls identified in this reference CP were intended to be appropriate for large, publicly-trusted CAs that issue certificates used to support TLS and code signing. While most material in this document should be appropriate for a wide range of applications, each community will need to tailor the specific controls identified by their CP as appropriate. This may involve adding and removing material from this reference CP as needed to accommodate the needs and constraints for their particular application, as well as modifying the controls as necessary to meet the assurance level required by the relying party community. A CPS may reference pre-existing documentation.

To help guide the CP writer, there are three types of information in this reference CP: suggested text, fill-in fields, and instructions. A section may contain any or all of these types of information.

> *Suggested text*: Most of the document is of this type. This text has been written to use without alteration. It represents a reasonable level of assurance for certificate issuance. The requirements reflect best business practices. However, the CP developer must consider his own organization's needs, resources, and capabilities carefully to ensure that all of the requirements, both those on the CA and on the organization itself, are adequate and can be met. Where appropriate, the suggested text can be altered, or can be replaced using the existing suggested text as an example.

> *Fill-in fields*: Some sections of the document contain fields where choices must be made by the CP writer, to tailor it for the intended purpose. These fields are denoted by <angle brackets>, and will contain an indication of the type of information that is to be filled in. The brackets contain a suggestion for the value to be filled in that is intended to be suitable for a moderate assurance system. The information supplied by the CP writer is intended to replace the fill-in field, including angle brackets.

> *Instruction:* There are a few areas of the CP that cannot be predicted and do not lend themselves to suggesting a generalized best practices requirement, nor are they such that a simple number must be selected. In this case, a paragraph will be supplied, that begins with an Instruction: tag and is in italic typeface. The instruction will give the CP writer information about how to complete the section, using existing organizational policy or documentation, or by creating other technical documents that will be referenced in the CP. These paragraphs are intended to be removed once the CP is completed.

Throughout this document key words are used to identify requirements. The key words "MUST", "MUST NOT", "SHALL", "SHALL NOT", "SHOULD", "SHOULD NOT", and "MAY" are used. These words are a subset of the IETF Request For Comments (RFC) 2119 key words, and have been chosen based on convention in other normative documents [RFC2119].

A primary objective for writing this document as a reference CP is to encourage better security practices for CAs. The as-is text is generally more detailed than a typical CP, particularly in areas such as network security. Compliance audits of processes, procedures and controls defined in CPSs against CPs based on this reference will serve to drive CA practices to a more secure, yet fully achievable, level.

1 Introduction

This document is intended to assist developers of Certificate Policies (CP) that are intended to control the issuance and management of public key certificates for specific organizations or applications. It is also intended to provide baseline requirements for secure certificate issuance, with special attention to network security best practices.

It has been written as a reference Certificate Policy, so that the CP developer can fill in sections specific to organizational needs and quickly produce a suitable CP. This Reference CP is consistent with the Internet Engineering Task Force (IETF) Public Key Infrastructure X.509 (IETF PKIX) Certificate Policy and Certification Practices Framework [RFC3647]. The recommendations are intended to support audit programs.

Instruction: For the actual CP, remove the paragraphs above and replace them with a description of the Subscribers, organization(s), or application(s) that drive the requirements for certificate issuance that are defined in the CP.

A PKI that uses this CP provides some or all of the following security management services:

- Key generation/storage
- Certificate generation, modification, re-key, and distribution
- Key escrow and recovery of private keys associated with encryption (e.g. key management, key establishment) certificates
- Certificate Status services including Certificate revocation list (CRL) generation and distribution
- Repository management of certificate related items
- Certificate token initialization/programming/management
- System management functions (e.g., security audit, configuration management, archive.)

CAs that issue certificates under this policy may operate simultaneously under other policies. CAs must not assert this policy in certificates unless they are issued in accordance with all the requirements of this policy.

1.1 Overview

A CA is a collection of hardware, software, personnel, and operating procedures that issue and manage public key certificates, also known as digital certificates. The public key certificate binds a public key to a named subject. This allows relying parties to trust signatures or assertions made by the subject using the private key that corresponds to the public key contained in the certificate.

A fundamental element of modern secure communications is establishing trust in public keys. This begins with a Relying Party obtaining a Subscriber's public key certificate that is issued by a trusted entity certifying that the public key belongs to that Subscriber. Subscriber certificates that are not trusted directly may become trusted through successive validation of a chain of CA certificates from the Subscriber's certificate to a trust anchor (typically a Root-CA public key). Trust anchors are explicitly trusted by Relying Parties. Relying parties are responsible for securely obtaining trust anchors and for securely managing their trust anchor store. Relying parties, including the Trust Anchor Managers should configure trust anchors with great caution and should give full consideration to the requirements of this CP and associated compliance annual audit requirements.

1 ## 1.2   Name and Identification

2 *Instruction: Policy Object Identifiers (OID)s are identifiers in certificates that can indicate the assurance*
3 *provided by a certificate for a particular purpose. Relying parties use these OIDs to decide whether to*
4 *rely on identify the policy provisions under which these specific certificates were issued. Unless there is a*
5 *pre-approved OID available, the governing policy authority must register an OID for the purpose of*
6 *identifying the application-specific Certificate Policy. Once registered or approved, the OID shall be*
7 *listed in this section of the CP. The CP may have multiple policy OIDs associated with it for different use*
8 *cases (e.g. software-based certificates vs. hardware-based certificates).*

9 ## 1.3   PKI Participants

10 This section identifies roles that are relevant to the administration and operation of CAs under this policy.

11 ### 1.3.1   PKI Authorities

12 *Instruction: In a canonical organizationally monolithic PKI, the certification authority is an absolute*
13 *authority for the assertion of attributes related to subscribers. Trust in such a CA derives from the fact*
14 *that the CA is the embodiment of PKI policy for the organization. Few real-life organizations fit the*
15 *textbook mold, however, and non-organizational PKIs can be a mishmash of authority, liability, and*
16 *application. Therefore, rather than defining the CA as the only PKI authority, this section defines a*
17 *number of authorities, designed to deconstruct the types of authorities that would typically be held by a*
18 *CA. These are not trusted roles (which are defined later in Section 5.2.1) but rather pure authorities that*
19 *can be assigned to roles or offices or vendors to best fit the PKI using application. The separation of*
20 *these authorities can support several purposes, including multi-party integrity (watching the watchers)*
21 *and outsourcing of PKI functions. Additional authorities may be identified and defined as appropriate.*

22 *Policy Authority:* This is the entity that decides that a set of requirements for certificate issuance and use
23 are sufficient for a given application. The Policy Authority (PA):

24 •   Establishes and maintains the Certificate Policy (CP).

25 •   Approves the establishment of trust relationships with external PKIs that offer appropriately
26   comparable assurance.

27 •   Ensures that all aspects of the CA services, operations, and infrastructure as described in the
28   CPS are performed in accordance with the requirements, representations, and warranties of
29   the CP.

30 *Trust Anchor Managers (TAMs):* Authorities who manage a repository of trusted Root CA Certificates.
31 They act on behalf of relying parties, basing their decisions on which CAs to trust on the results of
32 compliance audits. A TAM sets requirements for inclusion of a CA's root public key in their store. These
33 requirements are based on both security and business needs. The TAM has a duty to enforce compliance
34 with these requirements, for example, requirements around the supply of compliance audit results, on
35 initial acceptance of a root, and on an ongoing basis. TAMs will follow their normal practice of requiring
36 CAs to submit an annual compliance audit report. It is our intention that the requirements in this
37 document will be included in those compliance audit schemes. As specified in Section 5.7, the TAM will
38 require the CA to provide notification of a compromise, and in response, the TAM will take appropriate
39 action.

40 ### 1.3.1.1   Certification Authority

41 The CA is the collection of hardware, software and operating personnel that create, sign, and issue public

key certificates to subscribers. This includes centralized, automated systems such as card management systems. The CA is responsible for issuing and managing certificates including:

- Approving the issuance of all certificates, including those issued to subordinate CAs and RAs.
- Publication of certificates
- Revocation of certificates
- Generation and destruction of CA signing keys
- Establishing and maintaining the CA system
- Establishing and maintaining the Certification Practice Statement (CPS)

Certification Authority (CA) Administrators and Operation Staff: CA components are operated and managed by individuals holding trusted, sensitive roles. Specific responsibilities for these roles, as well as requirements for separation of duties, are described in Section 5.2.

Security Auditor: An individual who is responsible for auditing the security of CAs or Registration Authorities (RAs), including reviewing, maintaining, and archiving audit logs; and performing or overseeing internal audits of CAs or RAs. A single individual may audit both CAs and RAs. Security Auditor is an internal role that is designated as trusted.

1.3.1.2 Certificate Status Servers

PKIs may optionally include a service that provides status information about certificates on behalf of a CA through on-line transactions. In particular, PKIs may include Online Certificate Status Protocol (OCSP) responders to provide on-line status information. Such a service is termed a Certificate Status Server (CSS). Where the CSS is identified in certificates as an authoritative source for revocation information or issued a delegated Responder certificate, the operations of that authority are considered within the scope of this CP. A CSS shall assert all the policy OIDs for which it is authoritative. Examples include OCSP servers that are identified in the Authority Information Access (AIA) extension. OCSP servers that are locally trusted, as described in [RFC2560], are not covered by this policy.

1.3.2 Registration Authorities

The registration authorities (RAs) collect and verify each subscriber's identity and information that is to be entered into the subscriber's public key certificate. The RA performs its function in accordance with a CPS approved by the Policy Authority. The RA is responsible for:

- The registration process
- The identification and authentication process.

Registration Authority Staff: RA Staff are the individuals holding trusted roles that operate and manage RA components."

1.3.3 Trusted Agents

The trusted agent is a person who performs identity proofing as a proxy for the RA. The trusted agent records information from and verifies biometrics (e.g., fingerprints, photographs) on presented credentials for an applicant's identity on behalf of the RA. The CPS will identify the parties responsible for providing such services, and the mechanisms for determining their trustworthiness.

1.3.4 Subscribers

A subscriber is the entity whose name appears as the subject in an end-entity certificate (also known as a subscriber certificate), agrees to use its key and certificate in accordance with the certificate policy asserted in the certificate, and does not itself issue certificates. CAs are sometimes technically considered "subscribers" in a PKI. However, the term "subscriber" as used in this document refers only to those who request certificates for uses other than signing and issuing certificates or certificate status information.

1.3.5 Relying Parties

A Relying Party is an entity that relies on the validity of the binding of the Subscriber's name to a public key. The Relying Party uses a Subscriber's certificate to verify or establish the identity and status of the Subscriber. A Relying Party is responsible for deciding whether or how to check the validity of the certificate by checking the appropriate certificate status information. A Relying Party may use information in the certificate to determine the suitability of the certificate for a particular use.

1.3.6 Other Participants

The CAs and RAs operating under the CP may require the services of other security, community, and application authorities. The CPS will identify the parties responsible for providing such services, and the mechanisms used to support these services.

Instruction: One such participant is the Compliance Auditor. CAs are required to engage organizationally-independent parties to perform compliance audits on a regular basis. To be effective, it is expected that compliance auditors will have expertise in information security, cryptography, and PKI, risk mitigation strategies, and industry best practices.

1.4 Certificate Usage

1.4.1 Appropriate Certificate Uses

Instruction: The sensitivity of the information processed or protected using certificates issued by the CA will vary significantly. Organizations must evaluate the environment and the associated threats and vulnerabilities and determine the level of risk they are willing to accept based on the sensitivity or significance of the information. This evaluation is done by each organization for each application and is not controlled by the CP. Provide narrative that indicates the <u>intended</u> usage for the credentials issued by the CAs operating under this CP. Examples include: device authentication/security, code signing, human subscriber authentication/intent to sign, etc.

1.4.2 Prohibited Certificate Uses

Instruction: There may be instances where prohibitions are appropriate. If so, state them here.

1.5 Policy Administration

1.5.1 Organization Administering the Document

The Policy Authority is responsible for all aspects of this CP.

1.5.2 Contact Person

Instruction: Policy Authority should identify and provide contact information for an individual that can

1   *provide authoritative answers to questions that arise through the use of their CP.*

2   ### 1.5.3   Person Determining CPS Suitability for the Policy

3   The Policy Authority shall approve the CPS for each CA that issues certificates under the policy.

4   ### 1.5.4   CPS Approval Procedures

5   CAs issuing under the policy are required to be evaluated against all facets of the policy. The Policy
6   Authority shall work with a CA to minimize the use of waivers.

7   The Policy Authority shall make the determination that a CPS complies with the policy. The CA and RA
8   must meet all requirements of an approved CPS before commencing operations. The Policy Authority
9   will make this determination based on the nature of the system function, the type of communications, or
10   the operating environment.

11   In each case, the determination of suitability shall be based on an independent compliance auditor's
12   results and recommendations. See section 8 for further details.

13   ## 1.6   Definitions and Acronyms

14   See Appendices A and B.

1 **2   Publication and Repository Responsibilities**

2 **2.1   Repositories**

3 All CAs that issue certificates under this policy are obligated to post all CA certificates issued by or to the
4 CA and CRLs issued by the CA in a repository that is publicly accessible through all Uniform Resource
5 Identifier (URI) references asserted in valid certificates issued by that CA. CAs may optionally post
6 subscriber certificates in this repository, except as noted in section 9.4.2. To promote consistent access to
7 certificates and CRLs, the repository shall implement access controls and communication mechanisms to
8 prevent unauthorized modification or deletion of information.

9 **2.2   Publication of Certification Information**

10 **2.2.1   Publication of Certificates and Certificate Status**

11 The publicly accessible repository system shall be designed and implemented so as to provide <99%>
12 availability overall and limit scheduled down-time to <0.5%> annually. Where applicable, the certificate
13 status server (CSS) shall be designed and implemented so as to provide <99%> availability overall and
14 limit scheduled down-time to <0.5%> annually.

15 **2.2.2   Publication of CA Information**

16 The CP shall be publicly available. The CPS of the CA is not required to be published. However, a
17 summary or redacted CPS shall either be publicly available or available upon request.

18 **2.3   Time or Frequency of Publication**

19 An updated version of the CP will be made publicly available within <thirty> days of the incorporation of
20 changes. The CRL is published as specified in Section 4.9.7. All information to be published in the
21 repository shall be published promptly after such information becomes available to the CA. The CA shall
22 specify in its CPS time limits within which it will publish various types of information.

23 **2.4   Access Controls on Repositories**

24 The CA shall protect information not intended for public dissemination or modification. CA certificates
25 and CRLs in the repository shall be publicly available through the Internet. Direct and/or remote access
26 to other information in the CA repositories shall be determined by Policy Authority. The CPS shall detail
27 what information in the repository shall be exempt from automatic availability and to whom, and under
28 what conditions the restricted information may be made available.

1	**3 Identification and Authentication**

2   **3.1   Naming**

3   **3.1.1   Types of Names**

4   The CA shall assign an X.501 Distinguished Name (DN) to each subscriber. This DN may or may not
5   appear in a certificate field. Subscriber certificates may contain any name type appropriate to the
6   application.

7   **3.1.2   Need for Names to Be Meaningful**

8   Names used in certificates must represent an unambiguous identifier for the subject. Names shall be
9   meaningful enough for a human to identify the named entity, irrespective of whether the entity is a
10   person, machine, or process. Interpreting the name semantic may require a reference database (e.g.,
11   human resources directory or inventory catalog) external to the PKI.

12   *Instruction: Examples are:*

13   *Person Name*   *John Q. Public*

14   *Domain Name*   *publicinfo.agency.dept.gov*

15   *Machine Name*   *"manufacturer=DeviceCorp, model=DC-ABCD, serial=00098765"*

16   *Email Address*   *jqpubli@devicecorp.com*

17   *IP Address*   *192.168.100.75 (shall be a routable, permanent IP address)*

18   While the issuer name in CA certificates is not generally interpreted by relying parties, this CP still
19   requires use of meaningful names by CAs issuing under this policy. CA certificates that assert this policy
20   shall not include a personal name, but rather shall identify the subject as a CA and include the name-space
21   for which the CA is authoritative. For example:

22   c= country, o = Issuer Organization Name, cn =*OrganizationX CA-3*
23

24   The subject name in CA certificates must match the issuer name in certificates issued by the subject, as
25   required by [RFC5280].

26   *Instruction: If certificates are to be used in a broad context, for example on the Internet or organization-*
27   *wide, specialized or difficult to interpret names should be avoided. This section needs to define local,*
28   *name-space specific semantics to all names used. The semantic must enable a relying party to identify a*
29   *single real entity from the name.*

30   **3.1.3   Anonymity or Pseudonymity of Subscribers**

31   The CA shall not issue anonymous certificates. Pseudonymous certificates, if issued shall be identified as
32   such. CAs issuing pseudonymous certificates shall maintain a mapping of identity to pseudonym.

1 ### 3.1.4 Rules for Interpreting Various Name Forms

2 Rules for interpreting distinguished name forms are specified in X.501. Rules for interpreting e-mail
3 addresses are specified in [RFC 2822].

4 *Instruction: If there is a local, name-space specific name form that requires specialized interpretation,*
5 *describe it here. It cannot be assumed that an arbitrary CA will be able to produce a special name form,*
6 *nor that an arbitrary application will be able to interpret a special name in the desired way.*

7 ### 3.1.5 Uniqueness of Names

8 Each CA must ensure that each of its subscribers is identifiable by a unique name. Each X.500 name
9 assigned to a subscriber by a CA (i.e., in that CA's namespace) must identify that subscriber uniquely.
10 When other name forms are used, they too must be allocated such that each name identifies only one
11 subscriber of that CA. Name uniqueness is not violated when multiple certificates are issued to the same
12 entity. For certificates that assert names that do not identify individual people, an Authorized Agency
13 Representative (AOR) shall be identified as having responsibility for the certificate subject.

14 The CPS shall identify the method for the assignment of unique subject names.

15 ### 3.1.6 Recognition, Authentication, and Role of Trademarks

16 CAs operating under this policy shall not issue a certificate knowing that it infringes on the trademark of
17 another. The PA shall resolve disputes involving names and trademarks.

18 ## 3.2 Initial Identity Validation

19 ### 3.2.1 Method to Prove Possession of Private Key

20 In all cases where the party named in a certificate generates its own keys, that party shall be required to
21 prove possession of the private key, which corresponds to the public key in the certificate request.

22 *Instruction: For signature and encryption keys, this may be done by the entity using its private key to*
23 *create a Certificate Signing Request (CSR), which the CA will then validate. Other mechanisms that are*
24 *at least as secure as those cited here may be used. The CA shall ensure that any mechanism or procedure*
25 *used ties the private key to the identity being asserted by the subscriber.*

26 In the case where key generation is performed under the CA or RA's direct control, proof of possession is
27 not required.

28 ### 3.2.2 Authentication of Organization Identity

29 Requests for CA certificates shall include the CA name, address, and documentation of the existence of
30 the CA. Before issuing CA certificates, an authority for the issuing CA shall verify the information, in
31 addition to the authenticity of the requesting representative and the representative's authorization to act in
32 the name of the CA.

33 For subscriber organization certificates, the CA shall verify the existence of the organization by verifying
34 the identity and address of the organization and that the address is the subscriber's address of existence or
35 operation.

36 *Instruction: The PA will define procedures for verifying organization identity. Additional requirements*

that could be used for organizational identity proofing can be found at [CABF EV] Section 11 and [CABF Base] Section 11.

3.2.3 Authentication of Individual Identity

Instruction: Public key certificates bind public keys to identities. However, the entity to be identified depends on the application for which the public keys are used. For instance, in a banking transaction, a certificate may name a bank account holder (i.e., a person). When two networks pass information securely, each communicating part of the network may have a certificate that identifies the device providing the security. Identifying different types of entity requires different evidence and procedures. For each type of entity engaged in the applications that this policy supports, there must be a subsection here that details the required evidence and procedure. Five are included here: human, device, application or service, role holder, and code signer. Not all PKIs will support all entity types. PKIs may support entity types not included here.

3.2.3.1 Authentication of Human Subscribers

Instruction: The identity proofing requirements for individuals will vary based on local laws and the level of assurance the PKI is seeking to attain. The section below provides a baseline set of guidelines appropriate for issuing human subscriber certificates from publicly-trusted CAs.

The RA shall ensure that the subscriber's identity information is verified. Identity shall be verified no more than <30> days before initial certificate issuance. RAs may accept authentication of a subscriber's identity attested to and documented by a trusted agent or notary to support identity proofing of remote subscribers. Authentication by a trusted agent or notary does not relieve the RA of its responsibility to perform steps 1), 2), the verification of identifying information (e.g., by checking official records) in step 3), and the maintenance of records in step 4), below.

At a minimum, authentication procedures for human subscribers must include the following steps:

1) Verify that a request for certificate issuance to the applicant was submitted by the organization.
2) Verify Subscriber's organizational membership through use of official organization records.
3) Establish subscriber's identity by in-person proofing before the registration authority, based on the following process:
   a) The subscriber presents an official form of identification (e.g., an organization ID badge, a passport, or driver's license) as proof of identity
   b) The RA examines the presented credential that can be linked to the subscriber (e.g., a photograph on the credential itself or a securely linked photograph of applicant), and
   c) The credential presented above shall be verified by the RA for currency and legitimacy (e.g., the organization ID is verified as valid).
4) Verify information to be included in the certificate (e.g., e-mail address, subject alternative pseudonymous names).
5) Record and maintain records of the applicant by the RA or CA. This information is archived to help establish an audit trail for dispute resolution.

3.2.3.2 Authentication of Devices

Instruction: This section applies to identities assigned to hardware devices, not the software or applications that run on them. Such certificates can support automated inventory, for example.

Some computing and communications devices (routers, firewalls, etc.) will be named as certificate subjects. In such cases, an Authorized Organizational Representative (AOR), or in certain cases the device itself, must provide identifying information for the device. The AOR/device is responsible for providing registration information which may include:

- Equipment identification (e.g., serial number)
- Equipment certificate signing request CSR
- Equipment authorizations and attributes (if any are to be included in the certificate)
- Contact information to enable the CA or RA to communicate with the AOR when required.

The registration information provided by the AOR/device shall be verified. If the device itself provides this information, the identity of the device shall be authenticated. If the information is provided by an AOR for a single device or batch of devices, the AOR shall be authenticated.

Instruction: For example, the AOR may be authenticated by the CA or the RA using the procedures outlined in Section 3.2.3.1. Alternatively, the CA or RA may authenticate the AOR using an individual certificate issued under those procedures.

3.2.3.3 Authentication of Applications or Services

Instruction: This section applies to identities assigned to the services offered via a network, irrespective of the hardware running the software that implements the service. This enables services to be replaced from backup in the event of a hardware failure, without re-provisioning keys. (The hardware may have its own certificate, as described in Section 3.2.3.2 above.)

Some software applications or services will be named as certificate subjects. In such cases, an Authorized Organizational Representative (AOR) must provide identifying information for the device. The AOR is responsible for providing registration information which may include:

- Unique software application or service name (e.g. DNS name)
- Software application or service certificate signing request CSR
- Software application or service authorizations and attributes (if any are to be included in the certificate)
- Contact information to enable the CA or RA to communicate with the AOR when required.

The registration information provided by the AOR shall be verified. The CA shall validate that the AOR is authorized to request a certificate for the application or service.

Instruction: This may be done, for example, by checking the appropriate and reliable 3rd party database, or having the AOR demonstrate control of the domain. Additional requirements that could be used for application or service vetting can be found in [CABF EV] and [CABF Base].

3.2.3.4 Authentication for Role Certificates

A role certificate shall identify a specific role on behalf of which the subscriber is authorized to act rather than the subscriber's name. A role certificate shall not be a substitute for an individual subscriber certificate. Multiple subscribers can be assigned to a role at the same time.

Subscribers issued role certificates shall protect the corresponding role credentials to the same security level as individual credentials.

The procedures for issuing role certificates shall comply with all other stipulations of this CP (e.g., subscriber identity proofing, validation of organization affiliation, key generation, private key protection, and Subscriber obligations). The AOR may act on behalf of the certificate subject for certificate management activities such as issuance, renewal, re-key, modification, and revocation.

The CA or the RA shall record the information identified in Section 3.2.3.1 for an AOR associated with the role before issuing a role certificate. The CA or RA shall verify the identity of the AOR using an individual certificate in his or her own name issued by a CA with equivalent assurance as the role certificate, or other commensurate methods.

AORs shall be responsible for:

- Authorizing subscribers for a role certificate;
- Recovery of the private decryption key;
- Revocation of subscribers role certificates;
- Always maintaining a current up-to-date list of subscribers who are assigned the role; and
- Always maintaining a current up-to-date list of subscribers who have been provided the private keys for the role.

Instruction: When determining whether a role certificate is warranted, consider whether the role carries inherent authority beyond the job title. Role certificates may also be used for subscribers on temporary assignment, where the temporary assignment carries an authority not shared by the individuals in their usual occupation, for example: "Chair PKI Process Action Team".

3.2.3.5 Authentication for Code Signing Certificates

Instruction: Code signing indicates to the recipient of the code that the code comes from an authorized source, and that the integrity of the source has been protected during distribution (i.e., that the code hasn't been modified). A code signing certificate identifies the person or organization authorized to make those claims to the code recipient.

The procedures for issuing code signing certificates shall comply with all other stipulations of this CP (e.g., subscriber identity proofing, validation of organization affiliation, key generation, private key protection, and Subscriber obligations). One or more AORs shall be assigned to act on behalf of the code signing certificate subscriber for certificate management activities such as issuance, renewal, re-key, modification, and revocation.

The CA or the RA shall record the information identified in Section 3.2.3.1 for an AOR associated with the code signing certificate. The CA or RA shall verify the identity of the AOR using an individual certificate issued by a CA with equivalent assurance as the code signing certificate, or other commensurate methods.

AORs shall be responsible for:

- Authorizing subscribers for a code signing certificate
- Revocation of subscriber's code signing certificates
- Always maintaining a current up-to-date list of subscribers who are authorized to hold code signing certificates and their associated private keys.

3.2.4 Non-verified Subscriber Information

Information that is not verified shall not be included in certificates. All certificate contents are verified by the CA or RA, either directly or by an attestation from the AOR who is authoritative for the certificate subject.

3.2.5 Validation of Authority

Before issuing CA certificates or signature certificates that assert organizational authority, the CA shall validate the subscriber's authority to act in the name of the organization. For role certificates that identify subjects by their organizational roles, the CA shall validate that the individual either holds that role or has been delegated the authority to sign on behalf of the role.

An example of signature certificates that assert organizational authority is code signing certificates.

3.2.6 Criteria for Interoperation

Instruction: Describe in this section:

- *Whether interoperation between the CA(s) issuing certificates under this policy and other CA(s) is permitted*
- *Who makes the determination*
- *How the interoperation is accomplished (e.g., direct cross-certification bridge)- may be by reference to another document*

3.3 Identification and Authentication for Re-key Requests

3.3.1 Identification and Authentication for Routine Re-key

For re-key of any CA certificate issued under this certificate policy, identity may be established through use of current signature key, except that identity shall be established following the same procedures as the initial registration at least once every <number> years from the time of original registration.

For re-key of any subscriber certificate issued under this certificate policy, identity may be established through use of current signature key, except that identity shall be established following the same procedures as the initial registration at least once every <number> years from the time of original registration.

Instruction: In-person registration is considered to be more assured than one based on use of a previously certified key. Replace <NUMBER> in the previous paragraph with the number of years between mandatory in-person registrations. Once in 6 years is considered high assurance; once in 9 years is considered moderate assurance; once in 15 years is considered basic.

3.3.2 Identification and Authentication for Re-key after Revocation

In the event of certificate revocation, issuance of a new certificate shall always require that the party go through the initial registration process per Section 3.2 above.

3.4 Identification and Authentication for Revocation Request

Revocation requests must be authenticated. Requests to revoke a certificate may be authenticated using that certificate's public key, regardless of whether or not the associated private key has been compromised.

4 Certificate Life-Cycle Operational Requirements

4.1 Certificate Application

The Certificate application process must provide sufficient information to:

- Establish the applicant's authorization (by the employing or sponsoring organization) to obtain a certificate. (per Section 3.2.3)
- Establish and record identity of the applicant. (per Section 3.2.3)
- Obtain the applicant's public key and verify the applicant's possession of the private key for each certificate required. (per Section 3.2.1)
- Verify any role or authorization information requested for inclusion in the certificate.

These steps may be performed in any order that is convenient for the CA and applicants that does not compromise security, but all must be completed before certificate issuance.

4.1.1 Who Can Submit a Certificate Application

A certificate application shall be submitted to the CA by the Subscriber, AOR, or an RA on behalf of the Subscriber. Multiple certificate requests from one RA or AOR may be submitted as a batch.

4.1.2 Enrollment Process and Responsibilities

All communications among PKI Authorities supporting the certificate application and issuance process shall be authenticated and protected from modification; any electronic transmission of shared secrets and personally identifiable information shall be protected. Communications may be electronic or out-of-band. Where electronic communications are used, cryptographic mechanisms commensurate with the strength of the public/private key pair shall be used. Out-of-band communications shall protect the confidentiality and integrity of the data.

Subscribers are responsible for providing accurate information on their certificate applications.

4.2 Certificate Application Processing

Information in certificate applications must be verified as accurate before certificates are issued. Procedures to verify information in certificate applications shall be specified in the CPS.

4.2.1 Performing Identification and Authentication Functions

The identification and authentication of the subscriber shall meet the requirements specified for subscriber authentication as specified in Sections 3.2 and 3.3. The components of the PKI (e.g., CA or RA) that are responsible for authenticating the subscriber's identity in each case shall be identified in the CPS.

4.2.2 Approval or Rejection of Certificate Applications

Any certificate application that is received by a CA under this policy, for which the identity and authorization of the applicant has been validated, will be duly processed. However, the CA shall reject any application for which such validation cannot be completed, or when the CA has cause to lack confidence in the application or certification process.

1 *Instruction: This text presents a permissive approach to certificate issuance. For high-risk applications,*
2 *a more restrictive approach may be desired. In some organizations, there may be a policy authority to*
3 *whom to refer questionable cases.*

4.2.3 Time to Process Certificate Applications

5 Certificate applications must be processed and a certificate issued within <30 days> of identity
6 verification.

7 *Instruction: The time it takes to process a certification request can vary greatly, depending on*
8 *verification mechanisms. Device certificates might be issued instantly, while person certificates may be*
9 *delayed by employee database look-ups.*

4.3 Certificate Issuance

4.3.1 CA Actions during Certificate Issuance

12 Upon receiving the request, the CAs/RAs shall:

- Verify the identity of the requester as specified in Section 3.2.
- Verify the authority of the requester and the integrity of the information in the certificate request as specified in Section 4.1.
- Build and sign a certificate if all certificate requirements have been met (in the case of an RA, have the CA sign the certificate).
- Make the certificate available to the subscriber after confirming that the subscriber has formally acknowledged their obligations as described in Section 9.6.3.

20 The certificate request may already contain a to-be-signed certificate built by either the RA or the
21 subscriber. This certificate shall not be signed until all verifications and modifications, if any, have been
22 completed to the CA's satisfaction.

23 All authorization and other attribute information received from a prospective subscriber shall be verified
24 before inclusion in a certificate. The responsibility for verifying prospective subscriber data shall be
25 described in the CPS.

4.3.2 Notification to Subscriber by the CA of Issuance of Certificate

27 CAs operating under this policy shall inform the subscriber (or other certificate subject) of the creation of
28 a certificate and make the certificate available to the subscriber. For device certificates, the CA shall
29 issue the certificate according to the certificate requesting protocol used by the device (this may be
30 automated) and, if the protocol does not provide inherent notification, also notify the authorized
31 organizational representative of the issuance (this may be in batch).

4.4 Certificate Acceptance

33 Before a subscriber can make effective use of its private key, the CA shall explain to the subscriber its
34 responsibilities and obtain the subscriber's acknowledgement, as defined in Section 9.6.3.

4.4.1 Conduct Constituting Certificate Acceptance

36 Failure to object to the certificate or its contents shall constitute acceptance of the certificate.

1 *Instruction: This text is a generic acceptance test; it can be made stronger by tying the acceptance to the*
2 *acknowledgement of the user agreement if such acknowledgement is obtained in real-time.*

4.4.2 Publication of the Certificate by the CA

4 As specified in Section 2.1, all CA certificates shall be published in repositories.

5 This policy makes no stipulation regarding publication of subscriber certificates, except as noted in
6 Section 9.4.3.

4.4.3 Notification of Certificate Issuance by the CA to Other Entities

8 PKI Authorities must be notified whenever a CA operating under this policy issues a CA certificate.

9 *Instruction: It is important for an organization that has established a certification policy to know when*
10 *new sources of certificates that assert that policy come into being; this helps prevent rogue offerings.*

4.5 Key Pair and Certificate Usage

4.5.1 Subscriber Private Key and Certificate Usage

13 The intended scope of usage for a private key shall be specified through certificate extensions, including
14 the key usage and extended key usage extensions, in the associated certificate.

4.5.2 Relying Party Public Key and Certificate Usage

16 Certificates may specify restrictions on use through critical certificate extensions, including the basic
17 constraints and key usage extensions. All CAs operating under this policy shall issue CRLs specifying
18 the current status of all unexpired certificates except for OCSP responder certificates. It is recommended
19 that relying parties process and comply with this information whenever using certificates in a transaction.

4.6 Certificate Renewal

21 *Instruction: Renewing a certificate means creating a new certificate with the same name, key, and other*
22 *information as the old one, but with a new, extended validity period and a new serial number. Renewal of*
23 *a certificate does not require a change to the subjectName and does not violate the requirement for name*
24 *uniqueness.*

25 An old certificate may or may not be revoked, but must not be further re-keyed, renewed, or modified.

4.6.1 Circumstance for Certificate Renewal

27 Any certificate may be renewed if the public key has not reached the end of its validity period, the
28 associated private key has not been revoked or compromised, and the Subscriber name and attributes are
29 unchanged. In addition, the validity period of the certificate must not exceed the remaining lifetime of the
30 private key, as specified in Section 5.6. The identity proofing requirements listed in Section 3.3.1 shall
31 also be met.

32 CA Certificates and OCSP responder certificates may be renewed as long as the aggregated lifetime of the
33 public key does not exceed the certificate lifetime specified in Section 6.3.2.

34 The CA may renew previously-issued certificates during recovery from CA key compromise without

subject request or approval as long as the CA is confident of the accuracy of information to be included in the certificates.

4.6.2 Who May Request Renewal

For all CAs and OCSP responders operating under this policy, the corresponding operating authority may request renewal of its own certificate. The Subscriber, RA, LRA, or AOR may request the renewal of a Subscriber certificate.

4.6.3 Processing Certificate Renewal Requests

Digital signatures on subscriber renewal requests shall be validated before electronic renewal requests are processed per Section 3.3. Alternatively, subscriber renewal requests may be processed using the same process used for initial certificate issuance.

Instruction: Trust in the public key shall be established using certification path validation rules described in [RFC 5280], including validation of revocation status of each certificate in the path using current, valid revocation information (e.g, using a CRL whose nextUpdate field is later than the current, verification time).

4.6.4 Notification of New Certificate Issuance to Subscriber

The CA shall inform the subscriber of the renewal of his or her certificate and the contents of the certificate.

4.6.5 Conduct Constituting Acceptance of a Renewal Certificate

Failure to object to the renewal of the certificate or its contents constitutes acceptance of the certificate.

4.6.6 Publication of the Renewal Certificate by the CA

As specified in Section 2.1, all CA certificates shall be published in repositories.

Publication of renewed subscriber certificates is subject to the requirements in Section 2 and Section 9.4.3 of this policy.

4.6.7 Notification of Certificate Issuance by the CA to Other Entities

Instruction: There may be other entities, for example, certificate notaries, that should be notified when a certificate is issued. If so, list them here.

4.7 Certificate Re-key

Instruction: Re-keying a certificate consists of creating new certificates with a different public key (and serial number and key identifier) while retaining the remaining contents of the old certificate that describe the subject. The new certificate may be assigned a different validity period, specify a different CRL distribution point, and/or be signed with a different key. Re-key of a certificate does not require a change to the subjectName and does not violate the requirement for name uniqueness.

An old certificate may or may not be revoked, but must not be further re-keyed, renewed, or modified.

Subscribers shall identify themselves for the purpose of re-keying as required in section 3.3.

4.7.1 Circumstance for Certificate Re-key

Instruction: The longer and more often a key is used, the more susceptible it is to loss or discovery. Therefore, it is important that a subscriber periodically obtain new keys. (Section 6.3.2 establishes usage periods for private keys for both CAs and subscribers.) Examples of circumstances requiring certificate re-key include: expiration, loss or compromise, issuance of a new hardware token, and hardware token failure.

4.7.2 Who May Request Certification of a New Public Key

Requests for certification of a new public key shall be considered as follows:

- Subscribers with a currently valid certificate may request certification of a new public key.
- CAs and RAs may request certification of a new public key on behalf of a subscriber.
- For device, application/service, or role certificates, an AOR that owns or controls the device may request re-key.

4.7.3 Processing Certificate Re-keying Requests

Digital signatures on subscriber re-key requests shall be validated before electronic re-key requests are processed per Section 3.3. Alternatively, subscriber re-key requests may be processed using the same process used for initial certificate issuance.

Instruction: Trust in the public key shall be established using certification path validation rules described in [RFC 5280], including validation of revocation status of each certificate in the path using current, valid revocation information (e.g, using a CRL whose nextUpdate field is later than the current, verification time).

4.7.4 Notification of New Certificate Issuance to Subscriber

The CA shall inform the subscriber of the rekey of his or her certificate and the contents of the certificate.

4.7.5 Conduct Constituting Acceptance of a Re-keyed Certificate

Failure to object to the certificate or its contents constitutes acceptance of the certificate.

4.7.6 Publication of the Re-keyed Certificate by the CA

All CA certificates must be published as specified in Section 2

Publication of renewed subscriber certificates is subject to the requirements in Section 2 and Section 9.4.3 of this policy.

4.7.7 Notification of Certificate Issuance by the CA to Other Entities

Instruction: There may be other entities, for example, certificate notaries, that should be notified when a certificate is issued. If so, list them here.

4.8 Certificate Modification

Instruction: Modifying a certificate means creating a new certificate that has the same key, a different serial number, and that differs in one or more other fields from the old certificate. Because of the

1 *requirement to validate particular field changes, it is often simpler and more secure to require re-*
2 *certification than to offer certificate modification. This section should only be included if there is a well-*
3 *defined reason to offer certificate modification.*

4 An old certificate may or may not be revoked, but must not be further re-keyed, renewed, or modified.

4.8.1 Circumstance for Certificate Modification

6 A CA may perform certificate modification for a subscriber whose characteristics have changed (e.g.,
7 name change due to marriage). If the subscriber name has changed, the subscriber shall undergo the
8 initial registration process.

4.8.2 Who May Request Certificate Modification

10 Requests for certificate modification shall be considered as follows:

11 • Subscribers with a currently valid certificate may request certificate modification.
12 • CAs and RAs may request certificate modification on behalf of a subscriber.
13 • For device, application, and role certificates, an AOR may request certificate modification.

4.8.3 Processing Certificate Modification Requests

15 A certificate modification shall be achieved using one of the following processes:

16 • Initial registration process as described in Section 3.2
17 • Identification & Authentication using a subscriber-signed certificate modification request, as
18 described in Section 4.7.3. In addition, the validation of the changed subject information shall be
19 in accordance with the initial identity-proofing process as described in Section 3.2

20 The RA shall complete all required re-verification prior to issuing the modified certificate

4.8.4 Notification of New Certificate Issuance to Subscriber

22 The CA shall inform the subscriber of the modification of his or her certificate and the contents of the
23 certificate.

4.8.5 Conduct Constituting Acceptance of Modified Certificate

25 Failure to object to the certificate or its contents constitutes acceptance of the certificate.

4.8.6 Publication of the Modified Certificate by the CA

27 All CA certificates must be published as specified in section 2

28 Publication of renewed subscriber certificates is subject to the requirements in Section 2 and Section 9.4.3
29 of this policy.

4.8.7 Notification of Certificate Issuance by the CA to Other Entities

31 *Instruction: There may be other entities, for example, certificate notaries, that should be notified when a*
32 *certificate is issued. If so, list them here.*

1 ## 4.9 Certificate Revocation and Suspension

2 *Instruction: CAs operating under this policy should issue CRLs, and/or provide OCSP responses*
3 *covering all unexpired certificates issued under this policy except for OCSP responder. Relying party*
4 *client software may support on-line status checking and some support only CRLs.*

5 CAs operating under this policy shall make public a description of how to obtain revocation information
6 for the certificates they publish, and an explanation of the consequences of using dated revocation
7 information. This information shall be given to subscribers during certificate request or issuance, and
8 shall be readily available to any potential relying party.

9 Revocation requests must be authenticated. See Section 3.4 for more details.

10 ### 4.9.1 Circumstances for Revocation

11 *Instruction: Examples of circumstances that invalidate the binding are:*

12 - *Identifying information or affiliation components of any names in the certificate becomes invalid.*
13 - *Any information in the certificate becomes invalid.*
14 - *The subscriber can be shown to have violated the stipulations of its subscriber agreement.*
15 - *There is reason to believe the private key has been compromised.*
16 - *The original certificate request was not authorized.*
17 - *The subscriber or other authorized party (as defined in the CPS) asks for his/her certificate to be*
18 *revoked.*

19 *The list above is not intended to be an exhaustive list of circumstances for certificate revocation. Section*
20 *13.1.5 of the CAB Forum Baseline Requirements [CABF BASE] contains addition examples.*

21 A certificate shall be revoked when the binding between the subject and the subject's public key defined
22 within the certificate is no longer considered valid. When this occurs the associated certificate shall be
23 revoked and placed on the CRL and/or added to the OCSP responder. Revoked certificates shall be
24 included on all new publications of the certificate status information until the certificates expire.

25 ### 4.9.2 Who Can Request Revocation

26 Within the PKI, a CA may summarily revoke certificates within its domain. A written notice and brief
27 explanation for the revocation should subsequently be provided to the subscriber. The RA can request the
28 revocation of a subscriber's certificate on behalf of any authorized party as specified in the CPS. A
29 subscriber may request that its own certificate be revoked. The AOR of the organization that owns or
30 controls a device can request the revocation of the device's certificate. Other authorized individuals of the
31 organization may request revocation as described in the CPS.

32 ### 4.9.3 Procedure for Revocation Request

33 A request to revoke a certificate shall identify the certificate to be revoked and allow the request to be
34 authenticated (e.g., digitally or manually signed). The CA may request information sufficient to explain
35 the reason for revocation. The steps involved in the process of requesting a certification revocation are
36 detailed in the CPS.

1 ### 4.9.4 Revocation Request Grace Period

2 There is no grace period for revocation under this policy.

3 ### 4.9.5 Time within which CA must Process the Revocation Request

4 CAs will revoke certificates as quickly as practical upon receipt of a proper revocation request and after
5 the requested revocation time. Revocation requests shall be processed within <fours hours> of receipt.

6 ### 4.9.6 Revocation Checking Requirements for Relying Parties

7 *Instruction: Use of a revoked certificate could have damaging or catastrophic consequences in certain*
8 *applications. The matter of how often new revocation data should be obtained is a determination to be*
9 *made by the relying party.*

10 *If it is temporarily infeasible to obtain revocation information, then the relying party must either reject*
11 *use of the certificate or make an informed decision to accept the risk. Such use may occasionally be*
12 *necessary to meet an urgent operational requirement.*

13 ### 4.9.7 CRL Issuance Frequency

14 CRLs, if issued, shall be issued periodically per the CPS, even if there are no changes to be made, to
15 ensure timeliness of information. Certificate status information may be issued more frequently than the
16 issuance frequency described below.

17 Certificate status information shall be published no later than the next scheduled update. This will
18 facilitate the local caching of certificate status information for off-line or remote operation.

19 Online CAs that issue CRLs must issue them at least once every <24> hours, and the *nextUpdate* time in
20 the CRL may be no later than <96> hours after issuance time (i.e., the *thisUpdate* time).

21 Offline CAs that issue CRLs must issue CRLs at least once every <30> days, and the *nextUpdate* time in
22 the CRL may be no later than <60> days after issuance time (i.e., the *thisUpdate* time).

23 Circumstances related to emergency CRL issuance are specified in section 4.9.12.

24 *Instruction: If CRLs are issued, the frequency with which a CRL is issued is a trade-off between the*
25 *burden it places on issuing and validating systems, and giving Relying Parties the most up-to-date*
26 *revocation information. For highly sensitive applications, or where revocation is a common occurrence,*
27 *or where on-line status responses are constructed from CRL information, higher frequency is called for.*
28 *It is not generally considered a high burden for CAs to issue a daily CRL, nor for validating systems to*
29 *obtain a CRL that often (e.g., at the beginning of the business day).*

30 ### 4.9.8 Maximum Latency for CRLs

31 CRLs shall be published within <4> hours of generation. Furthermore, each CRL shall be published no
32 later than the time specified in the *nextUpdate* field of the previously issued CRL for same scope.

33 *Instruction: The time between CRL generation and publication must be minimized to be of use to Relying*
34 *Parties. A reasonable latency for the preceding paragraph is 4 hours; much shorter latency should be*
35 *routinely achievable in practice.*

4.9.9 On-line Revocation/Status Checking Availability

Where on-line status checking is supported, status information must be updated and available to relying parties within <24> hours of the decision to revoke.

Instruction: For OCSP responses to be credible, the time it takes from revocation to OSCP availability should be as short as possible. A reasonable number for the number in the preceding paragraph is 4 hours. A higher assurance PKI may require faster availability; 2 hours is recommended.

4.9.10 On-line Revocation Checking Requirements

Relying party client software should support on-line status checking. Client software using on-line status checking need not obtain or process CRLs.

4.9.11 Other Forms of Revocation Advertisements Available

Instruction: A CA may also use other methods to publicize the certificates it has revoked. Any alternative method must meet the following requirements:

- *The alternative method must be described in the CA's approved CPS;*
- *The alternative method must provide authentication and integrity services commensurate with the assurance level of the certificate being verified.*
- *The alternative method must meet the issuance and latency requirements for CRLs stated in Sections 4.9.7 and 4.9.8.*
- *Components involved in creation of revocation information including providing authentication and integrity services must meet the security requirements for CSS as stated in this CP.*

4.9.12 Special Requirements Related To Key Compromise

Instruction: It's extremely important that relying parties are made aware as soon as possible when a CA knows that there is no longer a one-to-one binding between a named entity and a private key. If a shorter time period is desired, list it here.

4.9.13 Circumstances for Suspension

Instruction: From the CA point of view, certificate suspension merely indicates some (undefined) level of doubt in the binding between subscriber name and key. From the Relying Party point of view, however, the certificate is considered to be revoked. Certificate suspension is not recommended unless there is a narrowly defined use-case and the intended Relying Party interpretation of the suspension is clearly communicated. In that case, RFC3647 includes additional sections to be completed. Certificate Status Services

Instruction: There is no requirement to operate a certificate status service, but it is perceived as more efficient and can provide more timely information if the service obtains CRLs more frequently than client applications. If the organization decides to offer such a service, these sections must be completed to allow Relying Parties to decide what can be inferred from the status information they receive.

4.10 End Of Subscription

Subscription is synonymous with the certificate validity period. The subscription ends when the certificate is revoked or expired.

1 **4.11 Key Escrow and Recovery**

2 **4.11.1 Key Escrow and Recovery Policy and Practices**

3 CA private keys shall never be escrowed.

4 Under no circumstances shall a subscriber signature key be held in trust by a third party. CAs that
5 support private key escrow for key management keys shall document their specific practices in their CPS
6 and key escrow documentation.

7 *Instruction: Subscriber key management keys may be escrowed to provide key recovery. Escrowed keys*
8 *shall be protected at no less than the level of security in which they are generated, delivered, and*
9 *protected by the subscriber.*

10 **4.11.2 Session Key Encapsulation and Recovery Policy and Practices**

11 *Instruction: CAs that support session key encapsulation and recovery shall identify the document*
12 *describing the practices in the applicable CPS. Components that support session key recovery shall meet*
13 *the security requirements for the CAs as stated in this CP.*

5   Facility, Management, and Operational Controls

5.1   Physical Controls

All CA and RA equipment, including cryptographic modules, shall be protected from theft, loss, and unauthorized access at all times. Unauthorized use of CA and RA equipment is prohibited. CA equipment shall be dedicated to performing CA functions. RA equipment shall be operated to ensure that the equipment meets all physical controls at all times.

Instruction: The following sections discuss the CA and the RA as if they were physically separate. If they are not, then the most strict of any applicable requirement must apply.

5.1.1   Site Location and Construction

The location and construction of the facility housing the CA equipment, as well as sites housing remote workstations used to administer the CAs, shall be consistent with facilities used to house high-value, sensitive information. The site location and construction, when combined with other physical security protection mechanisms such as guards, high security locks, and intrusion sensors, shall provide robust protection against unauthorized access to the CA equipment and records.

5.1.2   Physical Access

5.1.2.1   Physical Access for CA Equipment

Physical access to CA equipment shall be limited to CA Operations Staff and Security Auditors. The security mechanisms shall be commensurate with the level of threat in the equipment environment.

At a minimum, physical access controls for CA equipment and all copies of the CA cryptographic module shall meet the following requirements:

- Ensure that no unauthorized access to the hardware is permitted
- Be manually or electronically monitored for unauthorized intrusion at all times
- Ensure an access log is maintained and available for inspection.
- Mandate at least two-person access requirements. Both people must hold trusted roles and at least one individual shall be a member of the CA Operations Staff. Technical or mechanical mechanisms (e.g., dual locks) shall be used to enforce the two-person physical access control
- Other individuals shall be escorted by two persons. This includes maintenance personnel. All individuals shall be recorded in the access log.
- Upon the permanent departure of trusted personnel, ensure access to sensitive physical areas is denied.

When not in use, removable CA cryptographic modules, removable media, and any activation information necessary to access or enable CA cryptographic modules or CA equipment, or paper containing sensitive plain-text information shall be placed in locked containers sufficient for housing equipment and information commensurate with the sensitivity of the application being protected. Access to the contents of the locked containers shall be restricted to individuals holding CA trusted roles as defined in Section 5.2.1, utilizing two-person access controls, and two-person integrity while the container is unlocked.

CA cryptographic modules held within the work area for intermittent use throughout the day may be kept under one lock, as long as they are stored in an area where there are at least two persons physically present at all times. Knowledge of the combination or access to the key used to secure the lock shall be

1   restricted to authorized individuals only. When in active use, the cryptographic module shall be locked
2   into the system or container (rack, reader, server, etc.) using a physical lock under the control of the CA
3   Operations Staff to prevent unauthorized removal.

4   Any activation information used to access or enable the cryptographic modules or CA equipment shall be
5   stored separately from the associated modules and equipment. Such information shall either be
6   memorized or recorded and stored in a manner commensurate with the security afforded the associated
7   cryptographic module or equipment.

8   A security check of the room/rack housing CA equipment shall occur prior to leaving the room/rack
9   unattended by the CA Operations Staff. The check shall verify the following:

10 • The equipment is in a state appropriate to the current mode of operation (e.g., that cryptographic
11   modules are in place when "open", and secured when "closed")
12 • Any security containers are properly secured
13 • Physical security systems (e.g., door locks, vent covers) are functioning properly
14 • The area is secured against unauthorized access

15 If unattended, the facility housing CA equipment shall be protected by an intrusion detection system
16 (IDS).

17 If a facility is not continuously attended and does not include an IDS, a check shall be made at least once
18 every <24> hours to ensure that no attempts to defeat the physical security mechanisms have been made.
19 A person or group of persons shall be made explicitly responsible for making such checks. When a group
20 of persons are responsible, a log identifying the person performing a check at each instance shall be
21 maintained and secured. The last person to depart shall initial a sign-out sheet that indicates the date and
22 time, and asserts that all necessary physical protection mechanisms are in place and activated. The next
23 person to arrive shall inspect this log and raise a security incident if a required check was not completed.

24 ### 5.1.2.2 Physical Access for RA Equipment

25 RA equipment shall be protected from unauthorized access while the cryptographic module is installed
26 and activated. RAs shall implement physical access controls to reduce the risk of equipment tampering
27 even when the cryptographic module or physical token is not installed and activated. These security
28 mechanisms shall be commensurate with the level of threat in the RA equipment environment.

29 Any activation information used to access or enable the RA equipment shall be stored separately from the
30 associated modules and equipment. Such information shall either be memorized or recorded and stored in
31 a manner commensurate with the security afforded the associated cryptographic module or equipment.

32 ### 5.1.2.3 Physical Access for CSS Equipment

33 Physical access control requirements for CSS equipment (if implemented), shall meet the CA physical
34 access requirements specified in Section 5.1.2.1.

35 ### 5.1.3 Power and Air Conditioning

36 The CA shall have backup power capability sufficient to lock out input, finish any pending actions, and
37 record the state of the equipment automatically before lack of power or air conditioning causes a
38 shutdown. The backup power capabilities shall support the availability requirements in Section 6.7.3.

5.1.4 Water Exposures

CA equipment shall be installed such that it is not in danger of exposure to water (e.g., on tables or elevated floors).

Potential water damage from fire prevention and protection measures (e.g., sprinkler systems) are excluded from this requirement.

5.1.5 Fire Prevention and Protection

The CA shall comply with local commercial building codes for fire prevention and protection.

Instruction: For organizations that have specific fire prevention and protection mechanisms in place, these can be described here.

5.1.6 Media Storage

Media shall be stored so as to protect it from accidental damage (water, fire, electromagnetic) and unauthorized physical access. Media not required for daily operation or not required by policy to remain with the CA or RA that contains security audit, archive, or backup information shall be stored securely in a location separate from the CA or RA equipment.

Media containing private key material shall be handled, packaged, and stored in a manner compliant with the requirements for the sensitivity level of the information it protects or provides access. Storage protection of CA and RA private key material shall be consistent with stipulations in Section 5.1.2.

5.1.7 Waste Disposal

CA and Operations Staff and RA Staff shall remove and destroy normal office waste in accordance with local policy. Media used to collect or transmit privacy information shall be destroyed, such that the information is unrecoverable, prior to disposal. Sensitive media and paper shall be destroyed in accordance with the applicable policy for destruction of such material.

Destruction of media and documentation containing sensitive information, such as private key material, shall employ methods commensurate with those in [SP 800-88].

Instruction: Organizations should identify the specific policy that pertains to destruction of sensitive material. This could be documented in the CP or the CPS.

5.1.8 Off-Site Backup

A system backup shall be made when a CA system is activated. If the CA system is operational for more than a week, backups shall be made at least once per week. Backups shall be stored offsite. Only the latest backup needs to be retained. The backup shall be stored at a site with physical and procedural controls commensurate to that of the operational CA system.

The data backup media shall be stored in a facility approved for storage of information of the same value of the information that will be protected by the certificates and associated private keys issued or managed using the equipment with a minimum requirement of transferring, handling, packaging, and storage of the information in a manner compliant with requirements for sensitive material identified in Section 6.2.4.1.

1 **5.2 Procedural Controls**

2 **5.2.1 Trusted Roles**

3 A trusted role is one whose incumbent performs functions that can introduce security problems if not
4 carried out properly, whether accidentally or maliciously. Trusted role operations include:

5 • The validation, authentication, and handling of information in Certificate Applications
6 • The acceptance, rejection, or other processing of Certificate Applications, revocation requests,
7 renewal requests, or enrollment information
8 • The issuance, or revocation of Certificates, including personnel having access to restricted
9 portions of its repository
10 • Access to safe combinations and/or keys to security containers that contain materials supporting
11 production services
12 • Access to hardware security modules (HSMs), their associated keying material, and the secret
13 share splits of the PINs that protect access to the HSMs
14 • Installation, configuration, and maintenance of the CA
15 • Access to restricted portions of the certificate repository
16 • The ability to grant physical and/or logical access to the CA equipment

17 *Instruction: It is essential that the people selected to fill these roles shall be held accountable to perform*
18 *designated actions correctly or the integrity of the CA is weakened. The functions performed in these*
19 *roles form the basis of trust in the CA. This section requires two approaches to increase the likelihood*
20 *that these roles can be successfully carried out. The first approach minimizes the number of trusted roles*
21 *and ensures that the people filling those roles are trustworthy and properly trained. The second enforces*
22 *the concept of least privilege and distributes the functions of the roles among several people, so that any*
23 *malicious activity requires collusion.*

24 *The only trusted roles defined by this policy are the CA Administrators, CA Operations Staff, the RA Staff*
25 *and Security Auditors. Multiple people may hold the same trusted role, with collective privileges*
26 *sufficient to fill the role. CAs may use different titles to describe these roles, or break out the duties in*
27 *different ways, as long as the requirements for separation duties are met (see Sections 5.2.2 and 5.2.4).*
28 *Other trusted roles may be defined by the Organizational administering the PKI, in which case they will*
29 *be described as additional subsections below*

30 The CA shall maintain lists, including names, organizations, contact information, and organizational
31 affiliation for those who act in CA Administrator, CA Operations Staff, RAs, and Security Auditor trusted
32 roles, and shall make them available during compliance audits. The RA shall maintain lists, including
33 names, organizations, and contact information of those who act in RA Staff, RA Administrators, and RA
34 Security Auditor roles for that RA.

35 **5.2.1.1 CA Administrator**

36 *Instruction: Define the CA administrator role functions in this section. The CA administrator role is*
37 *typically responsible for:*

38 • *Installation, configuration, and maintenance of the CA and CSS (where applicable)*
39 • *Establishing and maintaining CA and CSS system accounts*
40 • *Configuring CA, RA, and CSS audit parameters*
41 • *Configuring CSS response profiles*

1   • *Generating and backing up CA and CSS keys*
2   • *Controlling and managing CA cryptographic modules*
3   • *System backups and recovery*
4   • *Changing recording media*
5   • *Posting Certificates and CRLs*

6   CA Administrators shall not issue certificates to subscribers.

7   ### 5.2.1.2   CA Operations Staff

8   The CA Operations Staff role is responsible for issuing certificates.

9   *Instruction: Define the CA Operations Staff role functions in this section. Typically, this includes:*

10   • *Registering new subscribers and requesting the issuance of certificates*
11   • *Verifying the identity of subscribers and accuracy of information included in certificates*
12   • *Approving and executing the issuance of certificates*
13   • *Requesting, approving and executing the revocation of certificates*
14   • *Approving infrastructure certificates issued to support the operations of the CA*
15   • *Approving revocation of certificates issued to CAs or to support the operations of the CA*
16   • *Approving certificates issued to RAs*
17   • *Authorizing RAs*
18   • *Approving revocation of certificates issued to RAs*
19   • *Providing Certificate revocation and suspension status information as part of a CSS (if*
20   *implemented)*
21   • *Generating Certificates and CRLs*
22   • *Configuring certificate profiles or templates*
23
24   *Note that the CA Operations Staff may act as an RA to register and vet subscribers.*

25   ### 5.2.1.3   Security Auditor

26   Security Auditors are responsible for internal auditing of CAs and RAs. This sensitive role shall not be
27   combined with any other sensitive role, e.g. the Security Auditor shall not also be part of the CA
28   Operations Staff or CA Administrator. Security Auditors shall review, maintain, and archive audit logs,
29   and perform or oversee internal audits (independent of formal compliance audits) to ensure that CAs and
30   RAs are operating in accordance with the associated CPSs.

31   ### 5.2.1.4   RA Staff

32   RA Staff are the individuals holding trusted roles that operate and manage RA components.

33   *Instruction: Define the RA Staff role functions in this section. RA Staff is typically responsible for the*
34   *following:*

35   • *Installation, configuration, and maintenance of the RA*
36   • *Establishing and maintaining RA operating system and application accounts*
37   • *Routine operation of the RA equipment such as system backup and recovery or changing*
38   *recording media*
39   • *Registering new Subscriber and requesting the issuance of certificates*

1 • *Verifying the identity of Subscribers*
2 • *Verifying the accuracy of information included in certificates*
3 • *Approving and executing the issuance of certificates*
4 • *Requesting, approving, and executing the suspension, restoration, and revocation of certificates*

5 **5.2.2 Number of Persons Required per Task**

6 Where multi-party control is required, all participants shall hold a trusted role. Multi-party control shall
7 not be achieved using personnel that serve in a Security Auditor role with the exception of audit
8 functions. The following tasks shall require two or more persons:

9 • Generation, activation, and backup of CA keys
10 • Performance of CA administration or maintenance tasks
11 • Archiving or deleting CA audit logs. At least one of the participants shall serve in a Security
12 Auditor role.
13 • Physical access to CA equipment
14 • Access to any copy of the CA cryptographic module
15 • Processing of third party key recovery requests

16 **5.2.3 Identification and Authentication for Each Role**

17 Individuals holding trusted roles shall identify themselves and be authenticated by the CA and RA before
18 being permitted to perform any actions set forth above for that role or identity. CA Operations Staff and
19 RA Staff shall authenticate using a credential that is distinct from any credential they use to perform non-
20 trusted role functions. This credential shall be generated and stored in a system that is protected to the
21 same level as the CA system.

22 CA and RA equipment shall require, at a minimum, strong authenticated access control for remote access
23 using multi-factor authentication. Examples of multi factor authentication include use of a password or
24 PIN along with a time-based token, digital certificate on a hardware token or other device that enforce a
25 policy of what a user has and what a user knows.

26 CA and RA equipment shall require, at a minimum, authenticated access control (e.g., strong passwords)
27 for local multi-party access.

28 Individuals holding trusted roles shall be appointed to the trusted role by an appropriate approving
29 authority. These appointments shall be annually reviewed for continued need, and renewed if
30 appropriate. The approval shall be recorded in a secure and auditable fashion. Individuals holding trusted
31 roles shall accept the responsibilities of the trusted role, and this acceptance shall be recorded in a secure
32 and auditable fashion.

33 Identity proofing of the RA shall be performed by a member of the CA Operations Staff.

34 Users shall authenticate themselves to all aspects of the network (servers, operating systems, applications,
35 databases, processes, etc.) before they can access that resource.

36 **5.2.4 Roles Requiring Separation of Duties**

37 Individuals serving as Security Auditors shall not perform or hold any other trusted role.

38 Only an individual serving in a Security Auditor role may perform internal auditing functions, with the

1 exception of those security audit functions (e.g., configuring, archiving, deleting) that require multi-
2 person control.

3 An individual that performs any trusted role shall only have one identity when accessing CA equipment.

4 5.3 Personnel Controls

5 Personnel Security plays a critical role in the CA facility's overall security system. Personnel Security
6 shall be designed to prevent both unauthorized access to the CA facility and CA systems and compromise
7 of sensitive CA operations by CA personnel.

8 *Instruction: Inadequate personnel security procedures or negligent enforcement of personnel security*
9 *policies can pose potentially devastating threats to security. These threats can include unauthorized*
10 *access, data loss and corruption, denial of service, and even facility sabotage and terrorism. Such events*
11 *can erode or destroy customer confidence in the CA.*

12 5.3.1 Qualifications, Experience, and Clearance Requirements

13 Personnel seeking to become Trusted Persons shall present proof of the requisite background,
14 qualifications and experience needed to perform their prospective job responsibilities competently and
15 satisfactorily.

16 Individuals appointed to any trusted role shall meet the following:

17 • Be employees of or contractor/vendor of the CA and bound by terms of employment or contract
18 • Be appointed in writing
19 • Have successfully completed an appropriate training program
20 • Have demonstrated the ability to perform their duties
21 • Have no other duties that would interfere or conflict with their responsibilities as defined in
22 Section 5.2.1
23 • Have not been previously relieved of trusted role duties for reasons of negligence or non-
24 performance of duties

25 5.3.2 Background Check Procedures

26 Persons fulfilling Trusted Roles shall pass a comprehensive background check. CAs shall have a process
27 in place to ensure employees undergo background checks at least every <5> years.

28 Prior to commencement of employment in a Trusted Role, the CA shall conduct background checks (in
29 accordance with local privacy laws) which include the following:

30 • Confirmation of previous employment
31 • Check of professional reference
32 • Confirmation of the highest or most relevant educational degree obtained
33 • Search of criminal records (local, state or provincial, and national)
34 • Check of credit/financial records
35 • Search of driver's license records
36 • Identification verification via National Identity Check (e.g., Social Security Administration
37 records), as applicable

38 Factors revealed in a background check that should be considered grounds for rejecting candidates for

Trusted Roles or for taking action against an existing Trusted Person generally include (but are not limited to) the following:

- Misrepresentations made by the candidate or Trusted Person
- Highly unfavorable or unreliable professional references
- Certain criminal convictions
- Indications of a lack of financial or personal responsibility

5.3.3 Training Requirements

All personnel performing duties with respect to the operation of the CA, CSS or RA shall receive comprehensive training. Training shall be conducted in the following areas:

- CA/CSS/RA security principles and mechanisms
- All PKI software versions in use on the CA/CSS/RA system
- All PKI duties they are expected to perform
- Disaster recovery and business continuity procedures
- Stipulations of this policy

5.3.4 Retraining Frequency and Requirements

All individuals responsible for PKI Trusted Roles shall be made aware of changes in the CA, CSS, RA operation. Any significant change to the operations shall have a training (awareness) plan, and the execution of such plan shall be documented. Examples of such changes are CA software or hardware upgrade, changes in automated security systems, and relocation of equipment.

Documentation shall be maintained identifying all personnel who received training and the level of training completed.

5.3.5 Job Rotation Frequency and Sequence

Instruction: Job rotation is not a pre-requisite for a CA. However, it can be valuable for organizations that want flexibility in the skill sets of their trusted role personnel. If an organization chooses to implement Job rotation it should be described here, to include the frequency of rotation, the measures taken to ensure trusted role boundaries are preserved, and the sequence of rotation (if any. If the organization chooses to forego job rotation, this can be marked "Not Applicable".

5.3.6 Sanctions for Unauthorized Actions

Appropriate administrative and disciplinary actions as documented in organization policy shall be taken against personnel who perform unauthorized actions (i.e., not permitted by this CP or other policies) involving the CA's systems, the certificate status verification systems, and the repository. Disciplinary actions may include measures up to and including termination and shall be commensurate with the frequency and severity of the unauthorized actions.

5.3.7 Independent Contractor Requirements

Contractor personnel filling trusted roles shall be subject to all requirements stipulated in this document. Independent contractors and consultants who have not completed or passed the background check procedures specified above shall be permitted access to the CA's secure facilities only to the extent they are escorted and directly supervised by people holding trusted roles at all times.

5.3.8 Documentation Supplied to Personnel

Documentation sufficient to define duties and procedures for each role shall be provided to the personnel filling that role.

5.4 Audit Logging Procedures

Audit log files shall be generated for all events relating to the security of the CAs, CSS, and RAs. Where possible, the security audit logs shall be automatically collected. Where this is not possible, a logbook, paper form, or other physical mechanism shall be used. All security audit logs, both electronic and non-electronic, shall be retained and made available during compliance audits.

5.4.1 Types of Events Recorded

Security auditing capabilities of CA, CSS, and RA operating system and applications shall be enabled during installation and initial configuration. At a minimum, each audit record shall include the following (either recorded automatically or manually for each auditable event):

- The type of event;
- The date and time the event occurred;
- Success or failure where appropriate, and
- The identity of the entity and/or operator that caused the event.

Time shall be synchronized with an authoritative time source to within <three minutes>.

A message from any source requesting an action by the CA, CSS or RA is an auditable event; the corresponding audit record must also include message date and time, source, destination, and contents.

The CA, CSS and RA shall record the events identified in the list below. Where these events cannot be electronically logged, the CA/CSS/RA shall supplement electronic audit logs with physical logs as necessary.

- SECURITY AUDIT:
  - o Any changes to the Audit parameters, e.g., audit frequency, type of event audited
  - o Any attempt to delete or modify the Audit logs
  - o Obtaining a third-party time-stamp
- IDENTIFICATION AND AUTHENTICATION:
  - o Successful and unsuccessful attempts to assume a role
  - o The value of maximum authentication attempts is changed
  - o Maximum unsuccessful authentication attempts occur during user login
  - o A CA Administrator unlocks an account that has been locked as a result of unsuccessful authentication attempts
  - o A CA Administrator changes the type of authenticator, e.g., from password to biometrics
  - o Attempts to set passwords
  - o Attempts to modify passwords
  - o Logon attempts to CA, CSS or RA applications
  - o Escalation of privilege
- LOCAL DATA ENTRY:
  - o All security-relevant data that is entered in the system
- REMOTE DATA ENTRY:
  - o All security-relevant messages that are received by the system

- DATA EXPORT AND OUTPUT:
  - o All successful and unsuccessful requests for confidential and security-relevant information
- KEY GENERATION:
  - o Whenever the CA generates a key. (Not mandatory for single session or one-time use symmetric keys)
- PRIVATE KEY LOAD AND STORAGE:
  - o The loading of Component private keys
  - o All access to certificate subject private keys retained within the CA for key recovery purposes
- TRUSTED PUBLIC KEY ENTRY, DELETION AND STORAGE:
  - o All changes to the trusted public keys, including additions and deletions
- SECRET KEY STORAGE:
  - o The manual entry of secret keys used for authentication
- PRIVATE AND SECRET KEY EXPORT:
  - o The export of private and secret keys (keys used for a single session or message are excluded)
- CERTIFICATE REGISTRATION:
  - o All certificate requests
- CERTIFICATE REVOCATION:
  - o All certificate revocation requests
- TOKEN MANAGEMENT
  - o Loading tokens with certificates
  - o Shipment of tokens
  - o Zeroizing tokens
- CERTIFICATE STATUS CHANGE APPROVAL:
  - o The approval or rejection of a certificate status change request
- CA/CSS/RA CONFIGURATION:
  - o Installation of the operating system
  - o Installation of the CA, CSS or RA
  - o Installing hardware cryptographic modules
  - o Removing hardware cryptographic modules
  - o Re-key of the CA, CSS or RA
  - o Destruction of cryptographic modules
  - o System startup
  - o Any security-relevant changes to the configuration of the CA, CSS or RA
- ACCOUNT ADMINISTRATION:
  - o Roles and users are added or deleted
  - o The access control privileges of a user account or a role are modified
  - o Appointment of an individual to a trusted role
  - o Designation of personnel for multi-party control
- CERTIFICATE PROFILE MANAGEMENT:
  - o All changes to the certificate profile
- REVOCATION PROFILE MANAGEMENT:
  - o All changes to the revocation profile
- CERTIFICATE REVOCATION LIST PROFILE MANAGEMENT:
  - o All changes to the certificate revocation list profile
- MISCELLANEOUS:
  - o Receipt of hardware / software
  - o Backing up CA, CSS or RA internal database

1   o Restoring CA, CSS or RA internal database
2   o File manipulation (e.g., creation, renaming, moving)
3   o Posting of any material to a repository
4   o Access to CA, CSS or RA internal database
5   o All certificate compromise notification requests
6   o Configuration changes to the CA, CSS or RA server involving:
7   ▪ Hardware
8   ▪ Software
9   ▪ Operating system
10   ▪ Patches
11   • PHYSICAL ACCESS / SITE SECURITY:
12   o Personnel access to room housing CA, CSS, or RA
13   o Access to the CA, CSS, or RA server
14   o Known or suspected violations of physical security
15   o Any removal or addition of equipment to the CA/CSS/RA enclosure. (Equipment sign-
16   out and return)
17   • ANOMALIES:
18   o Software error conditions
19   o Software check integrity failures
20   o Receipt of improper messages
21   o Misrouted messages
22   o Network attacks (suspected or confirmed)
23   o Equipment failure
24   o Electrical power outages
25   o Uninterruptible power supply (UPS) failure
26   o Obvious and significant network service or access failures
27   o Violations of certificate policy
28   o Violations of certification practice statement
29   o Resetting operating system clock

30 5.4.2 Frequency of Processing Log

31 The audit log shall be reviewed at least once every <30> days and before being archived. All significant
32 events shall be explained in an audit log summary. Actions taken as a result of these reviews shall be
33 documented.

34 Such reviews involve verifying that the log has not been tampered with and performing a thorough
35 examination of any alerts or irregularities in the logs. A statistically significant portion of the security
36 audit data generated by the CA, CSS and RA since the last review shall be examined. This amount will
37 be described in the CPS.

38 Real-time automated analysis tools should be used. All alerts generated by such a systems shall be
39 analyzed.

40 5.4.3 Retention Period for Audit Log

41 Audit logs shall be retained on-site for at least <60> days in addition to being archived as described in
42 section 5.5. The individual who removes audit logs from the CA system shall be an official different
43 from the individuals who, in combination, command the CA signature key. For the CSS and RA, a CA
44 Administrator other than the CSS operator or RA shall be responsible for managing the audit log.

5.4.4 Protection of Audit Log

The security audit data shall not be open for reading or modification by any human, or by any automated process, other than those that perform security audit processing.

Electronic logs shall be protected to prevent alteration and detect tampering. Examples include digitally signing audit records or the use of a data diode to transfer logs to a separate system to prevent modification after the log is written to media.

Physical logbooks shall implement controls to allow for the detection of the removal of pages or deletion of entries.

Security audit data shall be moved to a safe, secure storage location separate from the location where the data was generated.

CA/CSS/RA system configuration and procedures must be implemented together to ensure that only authorized people archive or delete security audit data. Procedures must be implemented to protect archived data from deletion or destruction before the end of the security audit data retention period (note that deletion requires modification access).

5.4.5 Audit Log Backup Procedures

Audit logs and audit summaries shall be backed up at least every <30> days. A copy of the audit log shall be sent off-site every <30> days.

5.4.6 Audit Collection System (Internal vs. External)

The audit log collection system may or may not be external to the CA/CSS/RA system. Automated audit processes shall be invoked at system or application startup, and cease only at system or application shutdown. Audit collection systems shall be configured such that security audit data is protected against loss (e.g., overwriting or overflow of automated log files). Should it become apparent that an automated audit system has failed; CA/CSS/RA operations shall be suspended until the security audit capability can be restored.

5.4.7 Notification to Event-Causing Subject

Instruction: Generally, there is no requirement to notify a subject that an event was audited. Real-time alerts are neither required nor prohibited by this policy. Organizations may make their own determination as to whether notifications are required and under what circumstances and specify it here. Otherwise indicate "None".

5.4.8 Vulnerability Assessments

See Section 6.7.7 for requirements on regular penetration testing.

5.5 Records Archival

Instruction: The contents of this section are based on general archiving guidelines. The CA system may be subject to other rules and regulations. Incorporate these rules and regulations in this section by reference.

1 ### 5.5.1 Types of Events Archived

2 CA/CSS/RA archive records shall be sufficiently detailed to determine the proper operation of the
3 CA/CSS/RA and the validity of any certificate (including those revoked or expired) issued by the CA. At
4 a minimum, the following data shall be recorded for archive:

5 • CA/CSS/RA accreditation (if applicable)
6 • Certificate policy
7 • Certification practice statement
8 • Contractual obligations
9 • Other agreements concerning operations of the CA/CSS/RA
10 • System and equipment configuration
11 • Subscriber identity authentication data as per section 3.2.3
12 • Documentation of receipt and acceptance of certificates (if applicable)
13 • Subscriber agreements
14 • Documentation of receipt of tokens
15 • All CRLs issued and/or published
16 • All Certificates issued
17 • All Audit logs
18 • Other data or applications to verify archive contents
19 • Compliance Auditor reports
20 • Any changes to the Audit parameters, e.g. audit frequency, type of event audited
21 • Any attempt to delete or modify the Audit logs
22 • All access to certificate subject private keys retained within the CA for key recovery purposes
23 • All changes to the trusted public keys, including additions and deletions
24 • Remedial action taken as a result of violations of physical security
25 • Violations of Certificate Policy
26 • Violations of Certification Practice Statement

27 *Instruction: The above list is not exclusive. Many other relevant CA operations events are recorded in*
28 *the audit logs, and archived with those logs.*

29 ### 5.5.2 Retention Period for Archive

30 Archive records must be kept for a minimum of <7> years and <6> months without any loss of data.

31 *Instruction: Retention periods may be governed by law in the location of the CA. For instance, for US*
32 *Federal agencies, minimum retention set by NARA is 10 years and 6 months. Organizations should*
33 *consult their local laws and organizational archive policies to determine the applicable time period for*
34 *archive of these records.*

35 ### 5.5.3 Protection of Archive

36 No unauthorized user shall be permitted to write to, modify, or delete the archive. For the CA and CSS,
37 the authorized individuals are Security Auditors. For the RA, authorized individuals are designated by
38 the CA administrator and must be someone other than the RA.

39 For the CA/CSS/RA, archived records may be moved to another medium. The contents of the archive
40 shall not be released except in accordance with sections 9.3 and 9.4. Records of individual transactions
41 may be released upon request of any subscribers involved in the transaction or their legally recognized

1   agents.

2   Archive media shall be stored in a safe, secure storage facility separate from the CA/CSS/RA with
3   physical and procedural security controls equivalent to or better than those of the CA/CSS/RA. If the
4   original media cannot retain the data for the required period, a mechanism to periodically transfer the
5   archived data to new media shall be defined by the archive site.

6   ### 5.5.4   Archive Backup Procedures

7   The CPS or a referenced document shall describe how archive records are backed up, and how the archive
8   backups are managed.

9   ### 5.5.5   Requirements for Time-Stamping of Records

10   CA/CSS/RA archive records shall be automatically time-stamped as they are created. The CPS shall
11   describe how system clocks used for time-stamping are maintained in synchrony with an authoritative
12   time standard.

13   ### 5.5.6   Archive Collection System (Internal or External)

14   Archive data shall be collected in an expedient manner.

15   ### 5.5.7   Procedures to Obtain and Verify Archive Information

16   Procedures, detailing how to create, verify, package, transmit, and store the CA archive information, shall
17   be published in the CPS or a referenced document.

18   ## 5.6   Key Changeover

19   To minimize risk from compromise of a CA's private signing key, that key may be changed often. From
20   that time on, only the new key will be used to sign CA and subscriber certificates. If the old private key is
21   used to sign OCSP responder certificates or CRLs that cover certificates signed with that key, the old key
22   must be retained and protected.

23   The CA's signing key shall have a validity period as described in section 6.3.2.

24   When a CA updates its private signature key and thus generates a new public key, the CA shall notify all
25   CAs, RAs, and subscribers that rely on the CA's certificate that it has been changed. When a CA that
26   distributes self-signed certificates updates its private signature key, the CA shall generate key rollover
27   certificates, where the new public key is signed by the old private key, and vice versa. This permits
28   acceptance of newly issued certificates and CRLs without distribution of the new self-signed certificate to
29   current users. Key rollover certificates are optional for CAs that do not distribute self-signed certificates.

30   ## 5.7   Compromise and Disaster Recovery

31   ### 5.7.1   Incident and Compromise Handling Procedures

32   CA organizations shall have an Incident Response Plan and a Disaster Recovery Plan.

33   *Instruction: For example, see [SP 800-61] for additional information on the preparation of an Incident*
34   *Response Plan.*

If compromise of a CA is suspected, certificate issuance by that CA shall be stopped immediately. An independent, third-party investigation shall be performed in order to determine the nature and the degree of damage. The scope of potential damage shall be assessed in order to determine appropriate remediation procedures. If a CA private signing key is suspected of compromise, the procedures outlined in Section 5.7.3 shall be followed.

In case of a CSS key compromise, all certificates issued to the CSS shall be revoked and the revocation information shall be published immediately in the most expeditious manner. Subsequently, the CSS shall be re-keyed.

The CA shall notify the trust anchor managers in the case of a root CA or notify the superior CA in the case of a subordinate CA if any of the following occur:

- Suspected or detected compromise of any CA system or subsystem
- Physical or electronic penetration of any CA system or subsystem
- Successful denial of service attacks on any CA system or subsystem
- Any incident preventing a CA from issuing and publishing a CRL or OCSP response prior to the time indicated in the *nextUpdate* field in the currently published CRL or OCSP response
- Suspected or detected compromise of a certificate status server (CSS) if
    o the CSS certificate has a lifetime of more than <72> hours; and
    o the CSS certificate cannot be revoked (e.g., an OCSP responder certificate with the *id-pkix-ocsp-nocheck* extension)

5.7.2 Computing Resources, Software, and/or Data Are Corrupted

When computing resources, software, and/or data are corrupted, CAs operating under this policy shall respond as follows:

- Notify trust anchor managers or the superior CA as soon as possible.
- Ensure that the system's integrity has been restored prior to returning to operation and determine the extent of loss of data since the last point of backup.
- Reestablish CA operations, giving priority to the ability to generate certificate status information within the CRL issuance schedule.
- If the CA signing keys are destroyed, reestablish CA operations as quickly as possible, giving priority to the generation of a new CA signing key pair.
- If the integrity of the system cannot be restored, or if the risk is deemed substantial, reestablish system integrity before returning to operation.

5.7.3 Entity (CA) Private Key Compromise Procedures

5.7.3.1 Root CA Compromise Procedures

In the case of the Root CA compromise, the CA shall notify the trust anchor managers and relying parties via public announcement, and any cross-certified PKIs, of the Root CA compromise so that they can revoke any cross certificates issued to the Root CA or any Subordinate CAs and notify all Subscribers and Relying Parties to remove the trusted self-signed certificate from their trust stores. Notification shall be made in an authenticated and trusted manner. Initiation of notification to the trust anchor managers and any cross-certified PKIs shall be made at the earliest feasible time and shall not exceed <24> hours beyond determination of compromise or loss unless otherwise required by law enforcement. Initiation of notification to relying parties and subscribers may be made after mediations are in place to ensure continued operation of applications and services. If the cause of the compromise can be adequately

1 addressed, and it is determined that the PKI can be securely re-established, the CA shall then generate a
2 new Root CA certificate, solicit requests and issue new Subordinate CA certificates, securely distribute
3 the new Root CA certificate, and re-establish any cross certificates.

5.7.3.2 Intermediate or Subordinate CA Compromise Procedures

5 In the event of an Intermediate or Subordinate CA key compromise, the CA shall notify the trust anchor
6 managers and Superior CA. The superior CA shall revoke that CA's certificate, and the revocation
7 information shall be published immediately in the most expedient, authenticated, and trusted manner but
8 within <18> hours after the notification. The Compromised CA shall also investigate and report to the
9 trust anchor mangers and Superior CA what caused the compromise or loss, and what measures have been
10 taken to preclude recurrence. If the cause of the compromise can be adequately addressed and it is
11 determined that the CA can be securely re-established, then, the CA shall be re-established. Upon re-
12 establishment of the CA, new Subscriber certificates shall be requested and issued.

13 For Subordinate CAs, when a Subscriber certificate is revoked because of compromise, suspected
14 compromise, or loss of the private key, a revocation notice as specified in Section 4.9, shall be published
15 at the earliest feasible time by the supporting CA, but in no case more than <6> hours after notification.

5.7.3.3 CSS Compromise Procedures

17 In case of a CSS key compromise, the CA that issued the CSS a certificate shall revoke that certificate,
18 and the revocation information shall be published immediately in the most expedient, authenticated, and
19 trusted manner. The CSS shall subsequently be re-keyed. If the CSS is self-signed and the CSS
20 certificate expiration is more than <7> days away, the CA shall immediately notify the trust anchor
21 managers, relying parties, and any cross-certified PKIs of the CSS compromise so that they can notify all
22 Subscribers and Relying Parties to remove trust in the CSS certificate from each Relying Party
23 application, and install the re-keyed certificate.

24 It is recommended that the CSS have certificates with shorter lifetimes. A shorter lifetime minimizes the
25 time that a compromised certificate is available.

5.7.3.4 RA Compromise Procedures

27 In case of an RA compromise, the CA shall disable the RA. In the case that an RA's key is compromised,
28 the CA that issued the RA certificate shall revoke it, and the revocation information shall be published
29 within <24> hours in the most expedient, authenticated, and trusted manner. The compromise shall be
30 investigated by the CA in order to determine the actual or potential date and scope of the RA
31 compromise. All certificates approved by that RA since the date of actual or potential RA compromise
32 shall be revoked. In the event that the scope is indeterminate, then the CA compromise procedures in
33 Section 5.7.3.2 shall be followed.

5.7.4 Business Continuity Capabilities after a Disaster

35 CAs shall be required to maintain a Disaster Recovery Plan. The CA Disaster Recovery Plan shall be
36 coordinated with any overarching Disaster Recovery Plan that the broader organization may have. The
37 Disaster Recovery Plan shall identify what procedures are in place to mitigate risks to environmental
38 controls, procedures for annual testing of processes to restore service, individuals on call for this type of
39 activity, and the order of restoral of equipment and services.

40 In the case of a disaster in which the CA equipment is damaged and inoperative, the CA operations shall

1   be re-established as quickly as possible, giving priority to the ability to revoke Subscriber's certificates.
2   If the CA cannot re-establish revocation capabilities prior to date and time specified in the *nextUpdate*
3   field in the currently published CRL issued by the CA, then the inoperative status of the CA shall be
4   reported to the trust anchor managers and Superior CA. The trust anchor managers and Superior CA shall
5   decide whether to declare the CA private signing key as compromised and re-establish the CA keys and
6   certificates, or allow additional time for reestablishment of the CA's revocation capability.

7   In the case of a disaster whereby a CA installation is physically damaged and all copies of the CA
8   signature key are destroyed as a result, the CA shall request that its certificates be revoked. The CA
9   installation shall then be completely rebuilt by re-establishing the CA equipment, generating new private
10   and public keys, being re-certified, and re-issuing all cross certificates. Finally, all Subscriber certificates
11   will be re-issued. In such events, any Relying Parties who continue to use certificates signed with the
12   destroyed private key do so at their own risk, and the risk of others to whom the data is forwarded, as no
13   revocation information will be available (if the CRL signing key was destroyed).

14   ## 5.8   CA or RA Termination

15   When a CA operating under this policy terminates operations before all certificates have expired, entities
16   shall be given as much advance notice as circumstances permit.

17   Prior to CA termination, notice shall be provided to all cross-certified CAs requesting revocation of all
18   certificates issued to it. In addition:

19   • The CA shall issue a CRL revoking all unexpired certificates prior to termination. This CRL
20   shall be available until all certificates issued by the CA expire.
21   • The CA, CSS, and RA shall archive all audit logs and other records prior to termination
22   • The CA, CSS, and RA shall destroy all private keys upon termination
23   • The CA, CSS, and RA archive records shall be transferred to an appropriate authority specified in
24   the CPS
25   • If a Root CA is terminated, the Root CA shall use secure means to notify the subscribers to delete
26   all trust anchors representing the terminated CA.

1 **6   Technical Security Controls**

2 **6.1   Key Pair Generation and Installation**

3 **6.1.1   Key Pair Generation**

4 **6.1.1.1   CA Key Pair Generation**

5 Cryptographic keying material used by CAs to sign certificates, CRLs or status information shall be
6 generated in cryptographic modules validated to [FIPS 140] Level 3, or some other equivalent standard.
7 Multi-party control is required for CA key pair generation, as specified in section 6.2.2.

8 CA key pair generation must create a verifiable audit trail demonstrating that the security requirements
9 for procedures were followed. The documentation of the procedure must be detailed enough to show that
10 appropriate role separation was used. An independent third party shall validate the execution of the key
11 generation procedures either by witnessing the key generation or by examining the signed and
12 documented record of the key generation.

13 **6.1.1.2   RA Key Pair Generation**

14 Cryptographic keying material used by RAs to sign request and authenticate to the CA shall be generated
15 in hardware cryptographic modules validated to [FIPS 140] Level 2, or some other equivalent standard.

16 **6.1.1.3   Subscriber Key Pair Generation**

17 Subscriber key pair generation shall be performed by either the subscriber, CA, or RA. If the CA or RA
18 generates subscriber key pairs, the requirements for key pair delivery specified in section 6.1.2 must also
19 be met.

20 Software or hardware cryptographic modules validated to [FIPS 140], or some other equivalent standard,
21 should be used to generate all subscriber key pairs, as well as pseudo-random numbers and parameters
22 used in key pair generation.

23 *Instruction: If subscriber hardware tokens are required, then signature keys must be generated on the*
24 *hardware token to support source authentication.*

25 **6.1.1.4   CSS Key Pair Generation**

26 Cryptographic keying material used by CSSes to sign status information shall be generated in [FIPS 140]
27 Level 3, or equivalent, validated cryptographic modules.

28 **6.1.2   Private Key Delivery to Subscriber**

29 If subscribers generate their own key pairs, then there is no need to deliver private keys, and this section
30 does not apply.

31 When CAs or RAs generate keys on behalf of the subscriber, then the private key must be delivered
32 securely to the subscriber. Private keys may be delivered electronically or may be delivered on a
33 hardware cryptographic module. In all cases, the following requirements must be met:

- Anyone who generates a private signing key for a subscriber shall not retain any copy of the signing key after delivery of the private signing key to the subscriber.
- The private key(s) must be protected from activation, compromise, or modification during the delivery process.
- The subscriber shall acknowledge receipt of the private key(s).
- Delivery shall be accomplished in a way that ensures that the correct keys and activation data are provided to the correct subscribers.
  - For hardware modules, accountability for the location and state of the module must be maintained until the subscriber accepts possession of it.
  - For electronic delivery of private keys, the key material shall be encrypted using a FIPS-approved cryptographic algorithm and key size at least as strong as the private key. Activation data shall be delivered using a separate secure channel.

The CA must maintain a record of the subscriber acknowledgment of receipt of the key.

6.1.3   Public Key Delivery to Certificate Issuer

Where key pairs are generated by the subscriber or RA, the public key and the subscriber's identity must be delivered securely (e.g., using TLS with approved algorithms and key lengths) to the CA for certificate issuance. The delivery mechanism shall bind the subscriber's verified identity to the public key.

6.1.4   CA Public Key Delivery to Relying Parties

The public key of a root CA shall be provided to the subscribers acting as relying parties in a secure manner so that it is not vulnerable to modification or substitution.

Instruction: Examples of acceptable methods for delivery of the public key include:

- *Secure distribution of self-signed certificates through secure out-of-band mechanisms;*
- *Comparison of the hash of the self-signed certificate against a hash value made available via authenticated out-of-band sources (note that hashes posted in-band along with the certificate are not acceptable as an authentication mechanism);*

When a CA updates its signature key pair, the key rollover certificates may be signed with the CA's current private key; in this case, secure out-of-band mechanisms are not required.

6.1.5   Key Sizes

This CP requires use of RSA PKCS #1, RSASSA-PSS, DSA, or ECDSA signatures; additional restrictions on key sizes and hash algorithms are detailed below. Certificates issued under this policy shall contain RSA or elliptic curve public keys.

All certificates that expire on or before December 31, 2030 shall contain subject public keys of at least 2048 bits for RSA/DSA, at least 256 bits for elliptic curve, and be signed with the corresponding private key.

All certificates that expire after December 31, 2030 shall contain subject public keys of at least 3072 bits for RSA/DSA, at least 256 bits for elliptic curve, and be signed with the corresponding private key.

CAs that generate certificates and CRLs under this policy should use the SHA-256, or SHA-384 hash algorithm when generating digital signatures. ECDSA signatures on certificates and CRLs shall be

1 generated using SHA-256 or SHA-384, as appropriate for the key length.

2 RSA signatures on CRLs that only provide status information for certificates that were generated using
3 SHA-1 may continue to be generated using SHA-1.

4 Where implemented, CSSs shall sign responses using the same signature algorithm, key size, and hash
5 algorithm used by the CA to sign CRLs.

6 ### 6.1.6 Public Key Parameters Generation and Quality Checking

7 Public key parameters shall always be generated and validated in accordance with [FIPS 186-4].

8 Elliptic Curve public key parameters shall always be selected from the set specified in section 7.1.3.

9 ### 6.1.7 Key Usage Purposes (as per X.509 v3 Key Usage Field)

10 The use of a specific key is constrained by the key usage extension in the X.509 certificate. All
11 certificates shall include a critical key usage extension.

12 Public keys that are bound into human subscriber certificates should be used only for signing or
13 encrypting, but not both. Human subscriber certificates that contain signature keys shall assert the
14 *digitalSignature* bit. Human subscriber certificates that contain RSA public keys that are to be used for
15 key transport shall assert the *keyEncipherment* bit. Human subscriber certificates that contain elliptic
16 curve public keys that are to be used for key agreement shall assert the *keyAgreement* bit.

17 Public keys that are bound into CA certificates shall be used only for signing certificates and status
18 information (e.g., CRLs). CA certificates whose subject public key is to be used to verify other
19 certificates shall assert the *keyCertSign* bit. CA certificates whose subject public key is to be used to
20 verify CRLs shall assert the *cRLSign* bit. CA certificates whose subject public key is to be used to verify
21 Online Certificate Status Protocol (OCSP) responses shall assert the *digitalSignature* bit.

22 Public keys that are bound into device, applications, and service certificates may be used for digital
23 signature (including authentication), key management, or both. Device certificates to be used for digital
24 signatures shall assert the *digitalSignature* bit. Device certificates that contain RSA public keys that are
25 to be used for key transport shall assert the *keyEncipherment* bit. Device certificates that contain elliptic
26 curve public keys that are to be used for key agreement shall assert the *keyAgreement* bit. Device
27 certificates to be used for both digital signatures and key management shall assert the *digitalSignature* bit
28 and either the *keyEncipherment* (for RSA) or *keyAgreement* (for elliptic curve) bit.

29 The *dataEncipherment, encipherOnly,* and *decipherOnly* bits shall not be asserted in certificates issued
30 under this policy. In addition, *anyExtendedKeyUsage* shall not be asserted in extended key usage
31 extensions.

32 ### 6.2 Private Key Protection and Cryptographic Module Engineering Controls

33 ### 6.2.1 Cryptographic Module Standards and Controls

34 CAs shall use a hardware cryptographic module validated to [FIPS 140] Level 3 (or higher), or some
35 other equivalent standard for signing operations. RAs shall use a hardware cryptographic module
36 validated to [FIPS 140] Level 2 (or higher), or some other equivalent standard for signing operations.

1 CSSes that provide status information shall use a cryptographic module validated to [FIPS 140] Level 3
2 (or higher), or some other equivalent standard for signing operations.

3 Subscribers should use a cryptographic module validated to [FIPS 140], or some other equivalent
4 standard, for all cryptographic operations.

5 6.2.2 Private Key (N of M) Multi-Person Control

6 A single person shall not be permitted to activate or access any cryptographic module that contains the
7 complete CA signing key. CA signing keys shall be backed up only under multi-party control. Access to
8 CA signing keys backed up for disaster recovery shall be under multi-party control. The names of the
9 parties used for multi-party control shall be maintained on a list that shall be made available for
10 inspection during compliance audits.

11 6.2.3 Private Key Escrow

12 CA private keys shall never be escrowed.

13 Subscriber key management keys may be escrowed to provide key recovery as described in section
14 4.12.1. If a device has a separate key management key certificate, the key management private key may
15 be escrowed. The private key associated with a certificate that asserts a *digitalSignature* key usage shall
16 not be escrowed.

17 6.2.4 Private Key Backup

18 6.2.4.1 Backup of CA Private Signature Key

19 The CA private signature keys shall be backed up under the same multiparty control as the original
20 signature key. At least one copy of the private signature key shall be stored off-site. All copies of the CA
21 private signature key shall be accounted for and protected in the same manner as the original. Backup
22 procedures shall be included in the CA's CPS.

23 6.2.4.2 Backup of Human Subscriber and Role Private Keys

24 Backed up human subscriber and role private keys shall not be stored in plaintext form outside the
25 cryptographic module. Storage must ensure security controls consistent with the protection provided by
26 the subscriber's cryptographic module and shall be under the control of the subscriber.

27 6.2.4.3 Backup of CSS Private Key

28 CSS private keys may be backed up. If backed up, all copies shall be accounted for and protected in the
29 same manner as the original.

30 6.2.4.4 Backup of Device, Application and Code Signing Private Keys

31 Device, application and code signing private keys may be backed up or copied, but must be held under the
32 control of the AOR. Backed up private keys shall not be stored in plaintext form outside the
33 cryptographic module. Backup copies shall be controlled at the same security level as the original
34 cryptographic module.

6.2.5   Private Key Archival

CA private signature keys and subscriber private signature keys shall not be archived. CAs that retain subscriber private encryption keys for business continuity purposes shall archive such subscriber private keys in accordance with Section 4.11.

6.2.6   Private Key Transfer into or from a Cryptographic Module

CA private keys may be exported from the cryptographic module only to perform CA key backup procedures as described in Section 6.2.4.1. At no time shall the CA private key exist in plaintext outside the cryptographic module.

All other keys shall be generated by a cryptographic module. In the event that a private key is to be transported from one cryptographic module to another, the private key must be encrypted during transport; private keys must never exist in plaintext form outside the cryptographic module boundary.

Transport keys used to encrypt private keys shall be handled in the same way as the private key.

Instruction: For CA private keys, this means key transport keys must be protected under multi-person control.

6.2.7   Private Key Storage on Cryptographic Module

Instruction: Cryptographic modules may store private keys in any form as long as the keys are not accessible without the use of an authentication mechanism that is in compliance with [FIPS 140] or equivalent standard. In most cases this entry can simply state "No stipulation beyond that specified in FIPS 140 (or equivalent standard).

6.2.8   Method of Activating Private Key

The subscriber must be authenticated to the cryptographic token before the activation of the associated private key(s). Acceptable means of authentication include but are not limited to passphrases, PINs or biometrics. Entry of activation data shall be protected from disclosure (i.e., the data should not be displayed while it is entered).

A device or application may be configured to activate its private key without requiring activation data, provided that appropriate physical and logical access controls are implemented for the device and its cryptographic token. The AOR shall be responsible for ensuring that the system has security controls commensurate with the level of threat in the device's environment. These controls shall protect the device's hardware, software, and the cryptographic token and its activation data from compromise.

6.2.9   Method of Deactivating Private Key

Cryptographic modules that have been activated shall not be available to unauthorized access. After use, the cryptographic module shall be deactivated, e.g., via a manual logout procedure or automatically after a period of inactivity as defined in the applicable CPS. CA cryptographic modules shall be removed and stored in a secure container when not in use.

6.2.10 Method of Destroying Private Key

Individuals in trusted roles shall destroy CA, RA, and CSS (e.g., OCSP server) private signature keys when they are no longer needed. Subscribers shall either surrender their cryptographic module to CA/RA personnel for destruction or destroy their private signature keys, when they are no longer needed or when the certificates to which they correspond expire or are revoked. Physical destruction of hardware is not required.

6.2.11 Cryptographic Module Rating

See section 6.2.1.

6.3 Other Aspects of Key Pair Management

6.3.1 Public Key Archival

The public key is archived as part of the certificate archival described in Section 5.5.

6.3.2 Certificate Operational Periods and Key Usage Periods

Instruction: Special consideration must be given when a CA issues certificates for multiple applications that have different validity periods, for instance S/MIME certificates and code-signing certificates. Each type of subscriber will have a different date past which it will not be able to obtain a certificate for the full validity period. Whether that timing is managed by the issuing CA or the subscriber is implementation dependent.

Instruction: Validation of a subscriber certificate requires the valid issuing CA's certificate. A subscriber certificate that is issued just before the expiration of the issuing CA's certificate will only validate during the short time that remains in the CA's certificate validity period, regardless of the validity period asserted in the subscriber certificate. Therefore, a rule-of-thumb is to stop issuing subscriber certificates with a CA private key one subscriber certificate validity period before the expiration of the issuing CA's certificate. Another way to think about this is that no subscriber certificate shall have an expiration date beyond the expiration date in the issuing CA's certificate.

The usage period for the Root CA key pair is a maximum of <25> years.

For all other CAs operating under this policy, the usage period for a CA key pair is a maximum of <12> years. The CA private key may be used to sign certificates for at most <9> years, but may be used to sign CRLs and OCSP responder certificates for the entire usage period. All certificates signed by a specific CA key pair must expire before the end of that key pair's usage period.

Instruction: Subscribers should be aware of applications that have long term uses. For instance, data that is stored with its original encryption or documents that are stored with their original digital signatures may require special processing because all of the keys and certificates originally used will have expired or exceeded their initial period of usefulness. Subscribers who engage in such applications must ensure that those applications can use expired certificates, or manage the storage of their data such that the original signatures and encryptions are not used.

Subscriber public keys in certificates other than code signing certificates have a maximum usage period of <3> years. Subscriber signature private keys have the same usage period as their corresponding public key. The usage period for subscriber key management private keys is not restricted.

Subscriber public keys in code signing certificates have a maximum usage period of <10> years. The private keys corresponding to the public keys in these certificates have a maximum usage period of <10>

years.

For OCSP responders operating under this policy, the maximum private key usage period is <3> years.

6.4 Activation Data

6.4.1 Activation Data Generation and Installation

CA activation data may be user-selected (by each of the multiple parties holding that activation data). If the activation data must be transmitted, it shall be via an appropriately protected channel, and distinct in time and place from the associated cryptographic module.

RA and subscriber activation data may be user-selected. The strength of the activation data shall meet or exceed the requirements for authentication mechanisms stipulated for Level 2 in [FIPS 140], or some other equivalent standard. If the activation data must be transmitted, it shall be via an appropriately protected channel, and distinct in time and place from the associated cryptographic module.

6.4.2 Activation Data Protection

Data used to unlock private keys shall be protected from disclosure by a combination of cryptographic and physical access control mechanisms. Activation data shall be either:

- memorized;
- biometric in nature; or
- recorded and secured at the level of assurance associated with the activation of the cryptographic module, and shall not be stored with the cryptographic module.

6.4.3 Other Aspects of Activation Data

Instruction: Any other relevant requirements regarding activation data should be specified here.

6.5 Computer Security Controls

6.5.1 Specific Computer Security Technical Requirements

6.5.1.1 Access Control

Access to information such as sensitive details about customer accounts, passwords, and ultimately, CA-related private keys should be carefully guarded, along with the machines housing such information.

6.5.1.1.1 Access Control Policy and Procedures

The CA shall create and document roles and responsibilities for each trusted role employee job function in the CPS. The CA shall create and maintain a mapping of these trusted roles and their associated responsibilities to specific employees and their accounts on CA and/or RA systems.

6.5.1.1.2 Account Management

Information system account management features shall ensure that users access only that functionality permitted by their role or function. All account types with access to information systems shall be documented along with the conditions and procedures to follow in creating new accounts. Groups and roles shall have a documented relationship to the business or mission roles involved in operating the CA.

Section 5.2.1 of this document defines roles and job functions for personnel that the CA will use when defining access control mechanisms. The CA shall employ the principle of least privilege when creating users and assigning them to groups and roles; membership to a group or role shall be justified based upon business need. The CA shall take appropriate action when a user no longer requires an account, their business role changes, or the user is terminated or transferred. The CA shall <annually> review all active accounts to match active authorized users with accounts, and disable or remove any accounts no longer associated with an active authorized user.

Automated systems shall be employed to maintain access for only those users who are still authorized to use the information system. After <30 days> of inactivity, an account shall be automatically disabled and attempts to access any deactivated account shall be logged.

All account administration activities shall be logged and made available for inspection by appropriate security personnel. Account administration activities that shall be audited include account creation, modification, enabling, disabling, group or role changes, and removal actions. See Section 5.4 for detailed requirements for these logs.

Guest/anonymous accounts for logon to information systems shall be prohibited. Accounts shall be assigned to a single user and shall not be shared.

6.5.1.1.3 Least Privilege

In granting rights to accounts and groups, the CA shall employ the principle of least privilege, allowing only authorized access for users (and processes acting on behalf of users) which are necessary to accomplish assigned tasks in accordance with organizational missions and business functions. The CA shall explicitly authorize access to accounts and groups for controlling security functions and security-relevant information. The CA shall authorize access to privileged commands and features of information systems only for specific, organization-defined compelling operational needs and documents the rationale for such access. The CA shall require that users of information systems with access to administrative privileges to utilize non-privileged accounts or roles when accessing non-privileged functions (such as reading email).

6.5.1.1.4 Access Control Best Practices

Instruction: This section should identify appropriate security best practices related to the use and maintenance of user and administrative accounts. The CP writer may, for example, require that CA systems notify users of their previous successful logon, and implement automated session locks after periods of inactivity. This section may also identify other mitigations, such as limiting browser use by administrators so that it is only associated with specific administrative activities requiring a browser in the system, blocking browser access of publicly available websites.

6.5.1.1.5 Authentication: Passwords and Accounts

When the authentication mechanism uses operator selectable passwords, strong passwords shall be employed, as defined in <organization password policy>. Passwords for CA authentication shall be different from non-CA systems.

Instruction: Use of passwords for authentication is discouraged because they can be difficult to remember and easy to guess. However, they remain the most common form of system access authentication. Organizations generally have a policy regarding passwords and their management; if so, this policy should be referenced. Features of a good password policy generally include:

- *at least 12 characters long*
- *a mix of uppercase and lowercase characters, numbers, and symbols*
- *no consecutive repeating characters (for example, RR or 55)*
- *not based on username, personal information, or dictionary words*
- *dissimilar to previous passwords*
- *regularly changed (for instance, every 90 days)*

The CA shall have the minimum number of user accounts that are necessary to its operation. Account access shall be locked after <number, usually 3 to 5> unsuccessful login attempts. Restoration of access shall be performed by a different person who holds a trusted role, or restore access after a timeout period.

6.5.1.1.6 Permitted Actions without Identification or Authentication

The CA shall document in the CPS a specific list of actions that can be performed on specifically enumerated information systems without identification or authentication, such as retrieving or verifying a published CRL from an Internet-accessible server or accessing a publicly available website. Furthermore, the organization shall document and provide supporting rationale in its security policy and procedures an enumerated list of user actions and systems not requiring identification or authentication (i.e., anonymous access).

6.5.1.2 System Integrity

6.5.1.2.1 System Isolation and Partitioning

CA systems shall be configured, operated, and maintained so as to ensure the continuous logical separation of processes and their assigned resources. This separation shall be enforced by

- physical and/or logical isolation mechanisms, such as dedicated systems or virtualization
- protecting an active process and any assigned resources from access by or interference from another process
- protecting an inactive process and any assigned resources from access by or interference from an active process
- ensuring that any exception condition raised by one process will have no lasting detrimental effect on the operation or assigned resources of another process

All trusted components should be logically separated from each other, and shall be logically separated from any untrusted components of the CA system. The CPS shall document how this logical isolation of components is accomplished.

Security critical processes shall be isolated from processes that have external interfaces. For example the CA signing processes shall be isolated from registration processes. The CPS shall outline how security critical processes are protected from interference by externally facing processes.

If there are system resources shared amongst trusted and/or untrusted processes, the underlying system(s) shall prevent any unauthorized and unintended information transfer between processes via those shared system resources.

The CA shall develop and document controlled procedures for transferring software updates,

48

1 configuration files, certificate requests, and other data files between trusted components.

6.5.1.2.2 Malicious Code Protection

The CA system shall employ malicious code protection mechanisms to mitigate the risk of malicious code on CA system components. Malicious code on trusted CA components could allow an attacker to issue fraudulent certificates, create a rogue intermediate or signing CA server, or compromise the availability of the system.

CA system components running standard operating systems that are not air-gapped from the Internet shall employ host-based anti-malware tools to detect and prevent the execution of known malicious code. These tools shall be configured to automatically scan removable media when it is inserted, as well as files received over the network. Introduction of removable media shall not cause automatic execution of any software residing on the media.

Anti-malware tools employed by a CA shall be properly maintained and updated by the CA. Anti-malware tools on networked systems shall be updated automatically as updates become available, or CA Administrators shall push updates to system components on a <weekly> basis. Anti-malware tools may be employed on air-gapped systems. If anti-malware tools are employed on air-gapped systems, the CA shall document in the CPS how these tools will be updated, including mitigations intended to reduce the risks of spreading malware and exfiltration of data off of compromised CA systems.

Anti-malware tools shall alert CA Administrators of any malware detected by the tools.

On system components that do not implement host-based anti-malware tools, the CA shall identify and employ other malicious code protection mechanisms to prevent the execution of malicious code, detect infected files or executables, and remediate infected systems. These mechanisms could include, but are not limited to, compensating physical protection on hosts, network-based malware detection tools at boundary points, application whitelisting, and manually scanning removable media by trusted CA personnel. The CA shall document all malware protection mechanisms in the CPS.

6.5.1.2.3 Software and Firmware Integrity

The CA shall employ technical and procedural controls to prevent and detect unauthorized changes to firmware and software on CA systems. Access control mechanisms and configuration management processes (see Section 6.5.1.1 and 6.6.2) shall ensure that only authorized CA Administrators are capable of installing or modifying firmware and software on CA systems.

Root and subordinate CA servers shall implement automated technical controls to prevent and detect unauthorized changes to firmware and software. Example technical controls include signature verification prior to firmware/software installation or execution (such as firmware protections that comply with [SP800-147] or [SP800-147B]), or hash-based white-listing of executables. Unauthorized software or firmware detected by these mechanisms should be blocked from executing. Any instances of unauthorized firmware or software detected by the system shall be logged, and CA Administrators shall be notified of these events.

6.5.1.2.4 Information Protection

The CA shall protect the confidentiality and integrity of sensitive information stored or processed on CA systems that could lead to abuse or fraud. For example, the CA shall protect customer data that could allow an attacker to impersonate a customer. The CA shall employ technical mechanisms to prevent unauthorized changes or accesses to this information, such as access control mechanisms that limit which users are authorized to view or modify files. Sensitive information stored on devices that are not physically protected from potential attackers shall be stored in an encrypted format.

6.5.2 Computer Security Rating

Instruction: A computer security rating for computer systems may be required. The rating could be based, for example, on the Common Criteria for Information Technology Security Evaluation, ISO/IEC 15408:1999. Any such requirements should be listed in this section.

6.6 Life Cycle Technical Controls

6.6.1 System Development Controls

The system development controls address various aspects related to the development and change of the CA system through aspects of its life-cycle.

The CA system shall be implemented and tested in a non-production environment prior to implementation in a production environment. No change shall be made to the production environment unless the change has gone through the change control process as defined for the system baseline.

In order to prevent incorrect or improper changes to the CA system, the CA system shall require multi-party control for access to the CA system when changes are made.

For any software developed by the CA, evidence shall be produced relating to the use of a defined software development methodology setting out the various phases of development, as well as implementation techniques intended to avoid common errors to reduce the number of vulnerabilities. Automated software assurance (i.e. static code analysis) tools shall be used to catch common error conditions within developed code. For compiled code, all compiler warnings shall be enabled and addressed or acknowledged to be acceptable. Input validation shall be performed for all inputs into the system.

Hardware and software procured to operate the CA shall be purchased in a fashion to reduce the likelihood that any particular component was tampered with (e.g., by ensuring the vendor cannot identify the PKI component that will be installed on a particular device). The hardware and software shall be verified as being that supplied from the vendor, with no modifications, and be the version intended for use. Hardware and software updates shall be purchased or developed in the same manner as original equipment, and shall be installed by trusted and trained personnel in a defined manner.

All data input to CA system components from users or other system components shall be validated prior to consumption by the receiving entity. Validating the syntax and semantics of system inputs (e.g., character set, length, numerical range, and acceptable values) verifies that inputs match the expected definitions for format and content.

6.6.2 Security Management Controls

A list of acceptable products and their versions for each individual CA system component shall be maintained and kept up-to-date within a configuration management system. Mechanisms and/or procedures shall be in operation designed to prevent the installation and execution of unauthorized software. A signed whitelist of the acceptable software for the system should be one of the ways to control the allowed software. A CA system shall have automated mechanisms to inventory on at least a

1 daily basis software installed on a system and alert operators if invalid software is found.

2 To reduce the available attack surface of a CA system, only those ports, protocols, and services that are
3 necessary to the CA system architecture are permitted to be installed or operating. The CA system shall
4 maintain a list of ports, protocols, and services that are necessary for the correct function of each
5 component within the CA system. There shall be automated mechanisms to monitor the running processes
6 and open ports against the permitted list.

7 To validate the integrity of the CA system, automated tools that validate all static files on a component
8 shall be in operation to notify operators when a protected file has changed.

9 The CA system shall establish and document mandatory configuration settings for all information
10 technology components which comprise the CA system. All configuration settings capable of automated
11 assessment shall be validated to be set according to the guidance contained within a documented security
12 configuration checklist on at least daily basis for powered on systems or next power-on for systems which
13 are not left powered-on.

14 ### 6.6.3 Life Cycle Security Controls

15 *Instruction: The timeframes suggested below are appropriate values for managing high-value*
16 *information systems. When selecting values organizations should consider the value of the information*
17 *system and the threats to those systems. Additionally, organizations should be flexible enough to respond*
18 *to new emerging threats and have the capability to perform the following activities on an as-needed basis.*

19 For flaw remediation, the CA shall scan all online CA systems for vulnerabilities using at least one
20 vulnerability scanner every <one week>. The use of multiple scanners on the most sensitive systems is
21 strongly encouraged.
22
23 Each vulnerability found shall be entered into a vulnerability tracking database, along with the date and
24 time of location, and shall be remediated within <72 hours>. Remediation shall be entered into the
25 vulnerability database as well (including date and time).
26
27 The CA shall monitor relevant notification channels on a <daily> basis for updates to packages installed
28 on CA systems (including networking hardware). CAs shall have a plan for receiving notification of
29 software and firmware updates, for obtaining and testing those updates, for deciding when to install them,
30 and finally for installing them without undue disruption. For critical vulnerabilities, the CA shall evaluate
31 and install the update within <24 hours>. For less critical vulnerabilities, the CA shall evaluate each
32 package to determine whether an update is required, and if so, that update shall be applied to all affected
33 CA systems within <48 hours>. A log shall be kept of the notifications, the decision to apply/not apply
34 including reason, and the application of relevant updates/patches.
35
36 From time to time, the CA may discover errors in configuration files, either because of human error,
37 source data error, or changes in the environment which have made an entry erroneous. The CA shall
38 correct such errors within <24 hours> of discovery, and shall document the reason for the error, and the
39 associated correction.
40
41 Remediation activities should not cause unavailability of revocation information.

42 ## 6.7 Network Security Controls

43 Many components of a CA are connected to each other and their customers via various forms of

1 networks. While it is necessary for connections to customers and administrative systems, care needs to be
2 taken to ensure those connections do not adversely impact the security of those components. Guidelines
3 for effective CA networking security are discussed in the following sections.

6.7.1 Isolation of Networked Systems

5 Communication channels between the network-connected CA components and the trusted CA processing
6 components shall be protected against attack. Furthermore, information flowing into these CA
7 components from the network-connected CA components shall not lead to any compromise or disruption
8 of these components.

9 The components of a CA requiring direct network connections shall be minimized. Those networked
10 components shall be protected from attacks through the use of firewalls to filter unwanted protocols
11 (utilizing access rules, whitelists, blacklists, protocol checkers, etc., as necessary). Data loss prevention
12 tools shall be employed to detect inappropriate leakage of sensitive information.

6.7.2 Boundary Protection

14 *Instruction: Describe the boundary protections between CA security zones here. The following sections*
15 *will describe boundary protections in the context of four zone types. The zones are not assumed to be*
16 *nested. They may be interconnected, but are independent. Zone boundaries are defined by limits of*
17 *authority over the security of the data processed within the boundary. Interconnection of two zones, even*
18 *at the same protection level, must be done in a way that respects the different authorities of the two zones.*
19 *The zones are:*

20 • *Special Access Zone (SAZ) - highly controlled network area for processing and storage of*
21 *especially high value data. It should be assumed that a network in this zone is not interconnected*
22 *to any other network.*
23 • *Restricted Zone (RZ) - controlled network area for sensitive data processing and storage.*
24 • *Operations Zone (OZ) - network area containing systems for routine business operations.*
25 • *Public Zone (PZ) - any network area that is not behind a protective boundary controlled by the*
26 *organization. Includes the public Internet and the public telephone network. Since there is no*
27 *presumed control over the Public Zone, there are no requirements for boundary protection.*

6.7.2.1 PKI Network Zones Overview

29 *Instruction: The following three sections describe the boundary of each zone type in the context of an*
30 *extended CA, including connections to systems that support but are not part of the CA. In each section,*
31 *define the network protections to be provided to PKI components by assigning them to the permitted*
32 *zone(s) for each component.*

33 *The following zone assignments represent typical and reasonable protection:*

34 *- A Root CA is expected to reside in a Special Access Zone with no network connection to any other*
35 *network at all.*

36 *- Subordinate CAs are expected to reside in one or more Restricted Zones, with connections allowed*
37 *from the Public Zone for RA Agent access and from the Operations Zone for business function access.*

38 *- The RA Server is expected to reside in a Restricted Zone distinct from the Restricted Zone occupied by*
39 *the CA Signing Servers.*

1   - *The RA Agent may reside in a Restricted, Operations, or Public Zone. While the RA Agent may use*
2   *special hardware and software to accomplish their tasks, the organization will have no control over the*
3   *RA Agent's workstation's network connection if it operates in the Public Zone. The data must be self-*
4   *protecting or session protected as it leaves the RA Agent's workstation.*

5   ### 6.7.2.2 Special Access Zone Boundary

6   *Instruction: A SAZ has no physical nor logical interconnection to any other network.*

7   • *Physical boundary protection measures shall include checks for network elements (cables,*
8   *routers, wireless equipment) that indicate interconnection.*
9   • *Physical boundary protection devices shall fail securely in the event of an operational failure.*
10   • *Incoming communication is limited to certificate signing requests, revocation requests, and*
11   *system maintenance data.*
12   • *Outgoing communication is limited to signed certificates, CRLs, and any data related to*
13   *monitoring and audit.*
14   • *Communication shall be accomplished by means of write-once media or media that is sanitized*
15   *on first use and between uses. Media shall be scanned after writing. The sanitization and*
16   *scanning shall take place on a device isolated and designated solely for this purpose.*
17   • *Auditing functions shall be enabled on systems in the SAZ, according to the requirements in*
18   *Section 5.4.*
19   • *Systems shall be physically isolated to separate platform instances and uniquely identified on*
20   *each subnet within SAZ boundary with managed interfaces.*

21   ### 6.7.2.3 Restricted Zone Boundary

22   *Instruction: An RZ has physical interconnections to other RZs, OZs, and potentially the PZ.*

23   • *Physical interconnections must be documented as to where they exist, for what purpose, and what*
24   *protections are provided.*
25   • *All physical systems shall identify and limit all systems to managed interfaces.*
26   • *All interconnections must be filtered based on origin, destination, and type.*
27   • *Physical boundary protection measures shall include checks for network elements (cables,*
28   *routers, wireless equipment) that indicate unauthorized interconnection.*
29   • *Physical boundary protection devices shall fail securely in the event of an operational failure.*
30   • *Connections with other RZs may be firewalled interconnections that maintain the security posture*
31   *of each RZ.*
32   • *Connections with OZs must be limited to specific protocols, and connections digitally*
33   *authenticated. If there is a Wireless Access Point in the OZ, a VPN Gateway shall be used to*
34   *connect to the Restricted Zone.*
35   • *Confidentiality shall be provided depending on the sensitivity of the information transferred and*
36   *the route of the connection.*
37   • *Connection with the PZ must be made through a bastion host that is hardened for exposure to a*
38   *hostile network environment. Such bastion hosts must be minimized in number and documented*
39   *as to location, purpose, and system and service configuration.*
40   • *Firewalls shall allow only those protocols necessary to perform a function and only from*
41   *recognized network origins by denying network traffic by default and allowing network traffic*
42   *only by exception (i.e., deny all, permit by exception).*
43   • *All communications shall be source authenticated and should be encrypted.*

- *Incoming communications shall be limited to certificate signing requests, CRL requests, key recovery requests, key escrow messages, revocation requests, responses from support systems (e.g., from a directory), and system maintenance data.*
- *Outgoing communications shall be limited to signed certificates, CRLs, key recovery data, revocation request responses, requests for subscriber authentication and authorization data, and any data related to monitoring and audit.*
- *Monitoring and auditing functions shall be enabled on the systems in the RZ, including network components where appropriate, according to the requirements in Sections 5.4 and 6.7.5.*
- *Indications that boundary protections have failed must be dealt with urgently (see Section 5.7).*
- *Wireless access points (WAP) shall NOT be allowed in the Restricted Zone at any time.*

6.7.2.4 Operational Zone Boundary

Instruction: An OZ has physical interconnections to other OZs, RZs, and the PZ.

- *Physical interconnections must be documented as to where they exist, for what purpose, and what protections are provided.*
- *All interconnections must be filtered based on origin, destination, and type.*
- *Physical boundary protection measures shall include checks for network elements (cables, routers, wireless equipment) that indicate unauthorized interconnection.*
- *Physical boundary protection devices shall fail securely in the event of an operational failure.*
- *Connections with RZs shall be driven by the RZ boundary protection requirements.*
- *Connections with other OZs may be firewalled router interconnections that maintain the security posture of each OZ.*
- *Connections with the PZ must be limited to specific protocols, and connections digitally authenticated.*
- *Confidentiality of any interconnection shall be provided depending on the sensitivity of the information transferred and the route of the connection.*
- *Firewalls shall allow only those protocols necessary to perform a function and only from recognized network origins by denying network traffic by default and allowing network traffic by exception (i.e., deny all, permit by exception).*
- *All communications shall be source authenticated and should be encrypted.*
- *Incoming and outgoing communications shall be limited to data related to the business of the organization, system maintenance data, and any data related to monitoring and audit.*
- *Monitoring and auditing functions shall be enabled on the systems in the OZ, including network components where appropriate, according to the requirements in Sections 5.4 and 6.7.5.*
- *Indications that boundary protections have failed must be dealt with promptly (see Section 5.7).*
- *Wireless Access Points (WAP) should NOT be allowed in the OZ unless the radio frequency can be physically contained with high assurance to systems isolated in the OZ of the building structure.*

6.7.3 Availability

CA systems shall be configured, operated, and maintained to maximize uptime and availability. Scheduled downtime shall be announced to Subscribers.

Instruction: Certificate request/issuing services need to be available, but can tolerate some down time. The required level of availability is determined by business and process considerations.

Services supporting revocation requests shall be configured and deployed in such a manner and capacity

1 that overall availability shall be maintained at a minimum of <99.9%>, with no single outage lasting
2 longer than <10> minutes. Additionally, such services shall be homed in a minimum of two
3 geographically independent locations with no single-points of failure (SPOFs – e.g., same backbone
4 provider), which could affect availability.

5 *Instruction: If revocation information is not available, or if revocation information is inaccurate, then a*
6 *Relying Party could be easily convinced to trust a revoked certificate. See Section 2.2.1 for requirements*
7 *on publication availability.*

6.7.3.1 Denial of Service Protection

9 CAs shall state acceptable methods to request revocation in their CPS. At least one of those methods
10 shall be out of band (i.e. network connectivity is not required).

11 CAs shall take reasonable measures to protect certificate request and issuing services from known DoS
12 attacks. The CA request and issuing availability required by a Subscriber application shall be stated in its
13 CPS.

6.7.3.2 Public Access Protections

15 *Instruction: "Public Access" in this section shall mean widespread, anonymous access.*

16 Personal Identity Information used in the identity proofing process shall be protected at all times in
17 accordance with local law and shall not be available to public access.

18 Revocation information and CA certificate information shall be made available in accordance with
19 Section 2 of this CP. However, individual subscriber certificates need not be made available for public
20 access.

21 CAs shall employ firewalls or air-gap procedures to protect privacy-sensitive information from public
22 access.

6.7.4 Communications Security

24 This section covers three forms of CA communication: Intra-CA communications, CA to RA
25 communications, and RA to Subscriber communications. While communications security is necessary
26 across all three forms of communication, the threats, vulnerabilities, and technological capabilities change
27 depending on the environment.

28
29 *Instruction:*
30 *Intra-CA Communications: This form includes communications between the components that make up the*
31 *certificate manufacturing and signing function. These components are generally contained within and*
32 *between the SAZ and one or more RZ.*

33 *At minimum this includes the certification authority workstation and hardware security module. If the CA*
34 *is part of a managed network, it may also include a domain controller, directory (e.g., LDAP server), and*
35 *perhaps other components. The SAZ is kept physically isolated from communications networks, therefore*
36 *all communications that involve the SAZ and another security zone will be air-gapped.*
37
38 *CA to RA Communications: This form includes communications between the CA and RA Workstation*

1   *during the certificate request process or when the RA initiates a certificate revocation. These*
2   *communications are between an RZ and one or more OZ.*
3
4   *RAs are generally co-located with Subscribers, so communications between the RA and CA will typically*
5   *be inter-network. Although this could be accomplished by using a virtual private network connection, that*
6   *level of relationship between the RA and CA is unusual and not assumed.*
7   *RA to Subscriber Communications: This stage includes appointment scheduling and notifications. These*
8   *communications are between an OZ and the PZ.*
9
10   *The fewest number of assumptions can be made about the RA to Subscriber environment, because of the*
11   *variety of models for this relationship, and the relative lack of control over the Subscriber. Where there*
12   *is no RA, this section shall be construed to provide CA to Subscriber communications security*
13   *requirements.*

14 6.7.4.1 Transmission Integrity

15   Source authentication and integrity mechanisms shall be employed to all certificate request, manufacture,
16   and issuance communications, including all related services irrespective of whether those services are
17   hosted on the same or different platform than the CA workstation. Communications between CAs and
18   RAs shall be mutually authenticated to detect changes to information during transmission.

19   Source authentication for RA to Subscriber communications may employ either online (cryptographic) or
20   offline methods. Offline RA to Subscriber communications shall be protected by traditional means that
21   are legally sufficient (e.g., ink signatures on paper). Initial Subscriber data that has been collected in an
22   unauthenticated or mutable manner shall be verified by the RA before the certificate request is created.

23 6.7.4.2 Transmission Confidentiality

24   Intra-CA communications that cross the physical protection barrier of the certificate-signing portion of
25   the CA system shall be confidentiality-protected. Services used by the CA system that are not
26   administered by the CA administrative staff shall provide protection commensurate with the CP.

27   Confidentiality of Subscriber data shall be maintained. CA to RA communications shall employ
28   encryption to prevent unauthorized disclosure of information during transmission. The level of protection
29   for RA to Subscriber communications shall be determined by the Subscriber (or the Subscriber's
30   organization); in any case, the RA shall be prepared to employ typical techniques for Internet
31   confidentiality (e.g., single-side authenticated TLS).

32 6.7.4.3 Network Disconnect

33   Network connection lifetimes between co-located services are driven by the traffic between them.
34   Connections should be terminated after a period of inactivity that is defined in the CA's CPS.

35   Network connections between CAs, RAs, and Subscribers shall be terminated at the end of the session or
36   after a period of inactivity. The length of the period of inactivity is defined in the CA's CPS. Keep-alive
37   and quick-reconnect mechanisms should not be employed, so that message replay and session hijacking
38   are avoided.

6.7.4.4 Cryptographic Key Establishment and Management

Cryptographic key management for network connections between CAs, RAs and Subscribers includes all aspects of cryptographic key life cycle: key generation, distribution, storage, access and destruction for both symmetric and asymmetric keys.

Key generation and management shall be performed in cryptographic modules that are validated to [FIPS-140] Level 1 or higher. Keys that are backed up for business continuity shall have protection comparable to the operational key. All cryptographic key management processes shall be described in the CA's CPS.

RAs shall employ key protection mechanisms implemented in a hardware cryptographic module validated to [FIPS 140], or some other equivalent standard (e.g., smart token).

Keys that protect the integrity and confidentiality of an enrollment session shall be generated and managed using cryptographic mechanisms implemented in a cryptographic module validated to [FIPS 140], or some other equivalent standard.

6.7.4.5 Cryptographic Protection

Cryptographic mechanisms implemented in a cryptographic module validated to [FIPS 140], or some other equivalent standard, shall be employed to detect changes to information during transmission of Intra-CA communications.

Communications between the CA and RA systems shall use cryptographic mechanisms that are implemented in a cryptographic module validated to [FIPS 140], or some other equivalent standard.

Cryptographic processes for RA to Subscriber communications shall be implemented in a cryptographic module validated to [FIPS 140], or some other equivalent standard.

6.7.4.6 Application Session Authenticity

For stateless connections between CAs, RAs and Subscribers, a unique, random session identifier for each session shall be generated. The session identifiers shall be validated for each request. Session identifiers shall be invalidated at logout to preserve session authenticity. A logout capability shall be provided with an explicit logout message that indicates the reliable termination of authenticated communications sessions. Session identifiers shall be invalidated after <30 minutes> of inactivity.

6.7.5 Network Monitoring

The CA shall be monitored to detect attacks and indicators of potential attacks. This includes intrusion detection tools.

6.7.5.1 Events and Transactions to be Monitored

The CA shall identify a list of essential information, transaction types and thresholds that indicate potential attacks. These events should include:

- Bandwidth thresholds
- Inbound and outbound communication events and thresholds
- Unauthorized network services
- CPU usage thresholds

- Certificate request thresholds from a single RA
- Access Control thresholds

6.7.5.2 Monitoring devices

A CA shall deploy intrusion detection tools and other monitoring devices with the CA to collect intrusion information and at ad hoc locations within the system to track specific types of transactions of interest to the organization. These monitoring devices shall be configurable to react to specific indications of increased risk or to comply with law enforcement requests. The devices shall alert security personnel when suspected unauthorized activity is occurring. These devices shall be network-based and should be also host-based. Only persons holding trusted roles shall manage the operating state of monitoring devices. The CA should utilize automated tools to support near real-time analysis of events and these tools should be integrated into access control and flow control mechanisms for rapid response to attacks.

6.7.5.3 Monitoring of Security Alerts, Advisories, and Directives

A CA shall monitor information system security alerts, advisories, and directives on an ongoing basis. The CA shall generate and disseminate internal security alerts, advisories, and directives as deemed necessary. The CA should employ automated mechanisms to make security alert and advisory information available throughout the organization as needed. The CA shall implement security directives in accordance with established time frames, or notifies the compliance auditor of the degree of noncompliance.

6.7.6   Remote Access/External Information Systems

Instruction: For operational reasons, there may be a need to perform remote management of some CA resources. The requirements in this section are meant to allow remote management while maintaining the desired security posture. Organizations that decide not to allow remote access to CA equipment will make that statement here and not include the following subsections.

6.7.6.1   Remote Access

Instruction: The organization should state that remote access to CA equipment is permitted and the circumstances for which it is permitted here.

6.7.6.2   Bastion Host

All access to CA signing systems and RA servers shall be mediated by a bastion host (i.e. a machine that presents a limited interface for interaction with the other elements of the CA). No direct access is permitted. The bastion host shall be patched regularly, maintained, and shall only run applications required to perform its duties.

6.7.6.3   Documentation

The CA shall document allowed methods of remote access to CA systems, including usage restrictions and implementation guidance for each allowed remote access method.

6.7.6.4   Logging

Logging shall be performed on the bastion host for each remote access session with the CA, consistent with Section 5.4. In particular, logs shall include date and time of the connection, the authenticated identity of the requestor, the IP address of the remote system and should also include the commands sent to the bastion host. Logs shall be maintained on a corporate audit server.

6.7.6.5 Automated Monitoring

Automated monitoring shall be performed on all remote sessions with the bastion host, and on all interactions between the bastion host and other CA systems. Upon detection of unauthorized access, the CA shall terminate the connection and log the event.

Instruction: The conditions, procedures, and responsibilities for this monitoring must be specified either in the CP or by reference.

6.7.6.6 Security of Remote Management System

Machines used for remote access to the CA system shall be either corporately managed (including patching) or shall be a machine dedicated to that purpose. In particular, it shall not be used as a personal machine for the remote user. The machine shall be maintained at the same level as the machines that it accesses (i.e. all policies on patching, virus scanning, etc. that are levied on the target systems shall apply to this machine as well). The CA should make use of Network Access Control technology to check the security posture of the remote machine prior to connecting it to the network. Remote Management of the CA system shall be the only use of Remote Access.

6.7.6.7 Authentication

Any machine used to access CA systems remotely shall require two or more factors of authentication. In particular, a hardware token shall be required. Authentication shall occur between the remote machine and the bastion host.

6.7.6.8 Communications Security for Remote Access

All communications between the remote access host and the CA system shall be protected by [FIPS 140], or some other equivalent standard, validated cryptography, as required for CA to RA communications in Section 6.7.4.5. Session identifiers shall be invalidated at logout to preserve session authenticity, as described in section 6.7.4.6, Session Authentication.

6.7.7 Penetration Testing

Penetration testing exercises both physical and logical security controls. Regularly performing this testing will allow a CA to mitigate and avoid vulnerabilities in their systems.

The CA System shall <biannually>, or whenever major system changes occur, conduct external and internal penetration tests to identify vulnerabilities and attack vectors that can be used to exploit enterprise systems. Penetration testing shall occur from outside the network perimeter (i.e., the Internet or wireless frequencies around an organization) as well as from within its boundaries (i.e., on the internal network) to simulate both outsider and insider attacks.

A standard method for penetration testing consists of:

- pretest analysis based on full knowledge of the target system;
- pretest identification of potential vulnerabilities based on pretest analysis;
- testing designed to determine exploitability of identified vulnerabilities.

1 Detailed rules of engagement shall be agreed upon by all parties before the commencement of any
2 penetration testing scenario. These rules of engagement are correlated with the tools, techniques, and
3 procedures that are anticipated to be employed by threat-sources in carrying out attacks. An
4 organizational assessment of risk guides the decision on the level of independence required for
5 penetration agents or penetration teams conducting penetration testing. Vulnerabilities uncovered during
6 penetration testing shall be incorporated into the vulnerability remediation process.

7 **6.8 Time-Stamping**

8 Asserted times shall be accurate to within three minutes. Electronic or manual procedures may be used to
9 maintain system time. Clock adjustments are auditable events (see Section 5.4.1).

1 **7   Certificate, CRL, and OCSP Profiles**

2 **7.1   Certificate Profile**

3 Certificates issued by a CA under this policy shall conform to the <profile document reference>.

4 *Instruction: Although it is possible to specify all of the requirements for certificate fields and values in*
5 *this section, it is more common to include a reference here to a separate document that includes those*
6 *requirements. That document, called a "profile" because it specifies acceptable options and values from a*
7 *more general document, is written by technical staff and often based on a standard such as [RFC 5280].*
8 *The sections here are provided for assessment by a knowledgeable but non-expert reader; these sections*
9 *must be edited to agree with the profile document. The profile document must be carefully written to*
10 *provide the necessary security and interoperability features.*

11 Each certificate issued by a CA shall be given a serial number consisting of a unique, positive integer, not
12 longer than 20 octets. They shall contain at least <20 bits> of random. Each certificate issued by a CA
13 shall be given a serial number consisting of a unique, positive integer, not longer than 20 octets.

14 **7.1.1   Version Number(s)**

15 The CA shall issue X.509 v3 certificates (populate version field with integer "2").

16 **7.1.2   Certificate Extensions**

17 *Instruction: [RFC 5280] provides a complete list of standard certificate extensions, with definitions and*
18 *acceptable values. Other documents define a variety of other useful extensions. Any certificate extensions*
19 *that are to be used in certificates issued under this policy (that are not described elsewhere in this*
20 *section) must be listed here, either incorporated by reference or identified by OID and ASN.1 definition,*
21 *with processing rules. Special consideration must be given to whether an extension is marked critical;*
22 *such marking reduces interoperability, but may be necessary to attain the desired security.*

23 The key usage extension (`keyUsage`) shall be marked as critical. Certificates shall assert the minimum
24 number of key usages required for functionality. Signature certificates shall assert *digitalSignature*.
25 Encryption certificates shall assert either *keyEncipherment* or *keyAgreement*. CA certificates shall assert
26 *keyCertSign* and *cRLSign*.

27 Certificates shall assert the minimum number of extended key usages (`extKeyUsage`) required for
28 functionality. The *anyExtendedKeyUsage* key purpose shall not be asserted.

29 The basic constraints extension (`basicConstraints`) shall be marked critical in CA certficates, and
30 the path length constraint should be set to <2>.

31 **7.1.3   Algorithm Object Identifiers**

32 *Instruction: The following is the set of acceptable algorithm OIDs. Organizations should remove those*
33 *algorithms that are not applicable to the operating environment. Organizations may need to add other*
34 *appropriate algorithms to these lists depending on their needs.*

35 Certificates issued under this CP shall use the following OIDs for signatures:

sha256WithRSAEncryption	{iso(1) member-body(2) us(840) rsadsi(113549) pkcs(1) pkcs-1(1) 11}
sha384WithRSAEncryption	{iso(1) member-body(2) us(840) rsadsi(113549) pkcs(1) pkcs-1(1) 12}
sha512withRSAEncryption	{iso(1) member-body(2) us(840) rsadsi(113549) pkcs(1) pkcs-1(1) sha512WithRSAEncryption(13)}
id-RSASSA-PSS	{iso(1) member-body(2) us(840) rsadsi(113549) pkcs(1) pkcs-1(1) 10}
ecdsa-with-Sha256	{iso(1) member-body(2) us(840) ansi-X9-62(10045) signatures(4) ecdsa-with-SHA2(3) 2}
ecdsa-with-Sha384	{iso(1) member-body(2) us(840) ansi-X9-62(10045) signatures(4) ecdsa-with-SHA2(3) 3}
sha256withDSA	{ joint-iso-itu-t(2) country(16) us(840) organization(1) gov(101) csor(3)nistalgorithm(4) hashalgs(2) 1 }

Where certificates are signed using RSA with Probabilistic Signature Scheme (PSS) padding, the OID is independent of the hash algorithm; the hash algorithm is specified as a parameter. If RSA signatures with PSS padding are used, then the the hash algorithms and OIDs specified below shall be used:

id-sha256	{joint-iso-itu-t(2) country(16) us(840) organization(1) gov(101) csor(3) nistalgorithm(4) hashalgs(2) 1}

Certificates issued under this CP shall use the following OIDs to identify the algorithm associated with the subject key:

id-dsa	{iso(1) member-body(2) us(840) x9-57(10040) x9cm(4) 1}
Id-ecPublicKey	{iso(1) member-body(2) us(840) ansi-x9-62(10045) public key-type (2) 1}
id-ecDH	{iso(1) identified-organization(3) certicom(132) schemes(1) ecdh(12)}
rsaEncryption	{iso(1) member-body(2) us(840) rsadsi(113549) pkcs(1) pkcs-1(1) 1}
dhpublicnumber	{iso(1) member-body(2) us(840) ansi-x942(10046) number-type(2) 1}

Where the certificate contains an elliptic curve public key, the parameters shall be specified as one of the following named curves:

ansip256r1	{iso(1) member-body(2) us(840) 10045 curves(3) prime(1) 7}
ansip384r1	{ iso(1) identified-organization(3) certicom(132) curve(0) 34 }

1

7.1.4 Name Forms

3   The subject field in certificates issued under this policy shall be populated with an X.500 distinguished
4   name as specified in section 3.1.1.

5   The issuer field of certificates issued under this policy shall be populated with a non-empty X.500
6   Distinguished Name as specified in section 3.1.1.

7.1.5 Name Constraints

8   The CAs should assert name constraints in CA certificates.

7.1.6 Certificate Policy Object Identifier

10   Certificates issued under this CP shall assert the following OID(s):

11   <id-policy-defined-in-this-document>::=<OID>

12   *Instruction: This section spells out how the requirements of this certificate policy are asserted in*
13   *certificates. The OID specified above is the OID specified in Section 1.2. If this document defines more*
14   *than one certificate policy (e.g., defines more than one level of assurance), then they would be listed here*
15   *with a requirement to include the OID matching the policy followed during certificate issuance. Very*
16   *rarely, policy OIDs from other documents may be included as well, for instance a certificate may meet the*
17   *requirements for a departmental business function as well as requirements for organizational network*
18   *authentication. It should be kept in mind that certificate policy OIDs are an assertion to the user of the*
19   *certificate (i.e., the Relying Party), and should reflect all that is true and only that which is true about the*
20   *certificate.*

7.1.7 Usage of Policy Constraints Extension

22   The CAs may assert policy constraints in CA certificates.

23   *Instruction: The CAs may assert policy constraints in CA certificates A common use of policy constraints*
24   *in CA certificates is to provide limits on what purpose a CA can be trusted. If this is desirable, include*
25   *that information here.*

7.1.8 Policy Qualifiers Syntax and Semantics

27   *Instruction: A common use of policy qualifiers is to provide location information (e.g., URI) for a*
28   *certificate policy. If this is desirable, include that information here.*

7.1.9 Processing Semantics for the Critical Certificate Policies Extension

30   Certificates issued under this policy shall not contain a critical certificate policies extension.

7.2 CRL Profile

32   CRLs issued by a CA under this policy shall conform to the CRL profile specified in <profile document
33   reference>.

1   *Instruction: The instruction in Section 7.1 addressing the profile document reference, applies to the CRL*
2   *Profile.*

3   **7.2.1   Version Number(s)**

4   The CAs shall issue X.509 Version two (2) CRLs.

5   **7.2.2   CRL and CRL Entry Extensions**

6   Detailed CRL profiles addressing the use of each extension are specified in <profile document reference>.

7   **7.3   OCSP Profile**

8   OCSP Responses issued by a CA under this policy shall conform to the OCSP profile specified in
9   <profile document reference>.

10   Certificate status servers (CSSs) operated under this policy shall sign responses using algorithms
11   designated for CRL signing.

12   *Instruction: The instruction in Section 7.1 addressing the profile document reference, applies to the*
13   *OCSP Profile.*

14   **7.3.1   Version Number(s)**

15   CSSs operated under this policy shall use OCSP version 1.

16   **7.3.2   OCSP Extensions**

17   Detailed CRL profiles addressing the use of each extension are specified in <profile document reference>.

8 Compliance Audit and Other Assessments

CAs shall have a compliance audit mechanism in place to ensure that the requirements of their CPS are being implemented and enforced.

8.1 Frequency or Circumstances of Assessment

CAs and RAs shall be subject to a periodic compliance audit at least once per year.

Instruction: The frequency of the compliance audit is directly linked to the risks and impacts associated with the PKI. PKI policy managers should consider the size of the subscriber community, the desired level of assurance, the use cases associated with the credentials, and the sensitivity of the information accessed or exchanged in determining the compliance audit frequency. If a policy manager determines that a different compliance audit period is appropriate, this section should be updated.

8.2 Qualifications of Assessor

The auditor must demonstrate competence in the field of compliance audits, and must be thoroughly familiar with the CA's CPS and this CP. The compliance auditor must perform such compliance audits as a regular ongoing business activity. In addition to the previous requirements, the auditor must be a certified information system auditor (CISA) or IT security specialist, and a PKI subject matter specialist who can offer input regarding acceptable risks, mitigation strategies, and industry best practices.

8.3 Assessor's Relationship to Assessed Entity

The compliance auditor either shall be a private firm that is independent from the entities (CA and RAs) being audited, or it shall be sufficiently organizationally separated from those entities to provide an unbiased, independent evaluation. To insure independence and objectivity, the compliance auditor must not have served the entity in developing or maintaining the entity's CA Facility or certificate practices statement. The Policy Authority shall determine whether a compliance auditor meets this requirement.

8.4 Topics Covered by Assessment

The purpose of a compliance audit is to verify that a CA and its recognized RAs comply with all the requirements of the current versions of the CA's CPS. All aspects of the CA/RA operation shall be subject to compliance audit inspections.

8.5 Actions Taken as a Result of Deficiency

When the compliance auditor finds a discrepancy between the requirements of this CP or the stipulations in the CPS and the design, operation, or maintenance of the PKI, the following actions shall be performed:

- The compliance auditor shall note the discrepancy
- The compliance auditor shall notify the parties identified in section 8.6 of the discrepancy
- The party responsible for correcting the discrepancy will propose a remedy, including expected time for completion, to the appropriate PKI Authorities, as defined in Section 1.3.1.

Depending upon the nature and severity of the discrepancy, and how quickly it can be corrected, the Policy Authority may decide to temporarily halt operation of the CA or RA, to revoke a certificate issued to the CA or RA, or take other actions it deems appropriate. The Policy Authority shall provide to the CA

1   its procedures for making and implementing such determinations..

2   **8.6   Communication of Results**

3   An Audit Compliance Report shall be provided to the entity responsible for CA operations. The Audit
4   Compliance Report and identification of corrective measures shall be provided to the appropriate PKI
5   Authorities within <30> days of completion. A special compliance audit may be required to confirm the
6   implementation and effectiveness of the remedy.

9   Other Business and Legal Matters

9.1   Fees

9.1.1   Certificate Issuance or Renewal Fees

Instruction: Each organization will determine the issuance and renewal fees for its constituency if any. For PKIs that do not charge fees for the credentials being issued, this may be "Not Applicable."

9.1.2   Certificate Access Fees

Section 2.4 of this policy requires that CA certificates and CRLs be publicly available. CAs operating under this policy must not charge additional fees for access to this information.

9.1.3   Revocation or Status Information Access Fees

CAs operating under this policy must not charge additional fees for access to CRLs and OCSP status information.

9.1.4   Fees for other Services

Instruction: Individual PKI providers will determine fee structures and the services for which fees will be charged. This information will be placed in this section. For organizations that do not charge any fees for PKI services, this entry may be "Not Applicable."

9.1.5   Refund Policy

Instruction: PKI services made commercially available should explain the circumstances and procedures for providing refunds in this section. Alternatively, for Organizations that do not charge for services, this entry may be "Not Applicable".

9.2   Financial Responsibility

This CP contains no limits on the use of certificates issued by CAs under the policy. Rather, entities, acting as relying parties, shall determine what financial limits, if any, they wish to impose for certificates used to consummate a transaction.

9.2.1   Insurance Coverage

Instruction: Organizations whose PKI services are insured against loss/liability claims will describe that coverage here. Alternatively, this may be "Not Applicable".

9.2.2   Other Assets

Instruction: Any other assets associated with the PKI service that may be included in a financial settlement should be described here. Otherwise, this section is "Not Applicable."

9.2.3   Insurance or Warranty Coverage for End-Entities

Instruction: PKI service organization will describe any insurance or warranty coverage provided to subscriber organizations and individuals. If none, this section may be noted as such.

9.3 Confidentiality of Business Information

The CA shall protect the confidentiality of sensitive business information stored or processed on CA systems that could lead to abuse or fraud. For example, the CA shall protect customer data that could allow an attacker to impersonate a customer.

Public access to CA organizational information shall be determined by the CA.

9.4 Privacy of Personal Information

9.4.1 Privacy Plan

The CA shall develop, implement and maintain a privacy plan. The privacy plan shall document what personally identifiable information is collected, how it is stored and processed, and under what conditions the information may be disclosed.

9.4.2 Information Treated as Private

CAs shall protect all subscriber personally identifiable information from unauthorized disclosure. Records of individual transactions may be released upon request of any subscribers involved in the transaction or their legally recognized agents. The contents of the archives maintained by CAs operating under this policy shall not be released except as allowed by the privacy plan.

9.4.3 Information not Deemed Private

Information included in certificates shall not be deemed private, and will not be subject to the protections outlined in Section 9.4.2.

9.4.4 Responsibility to Protect Private Information

Sensitive information must be stored securely, and may be released only in accordance with other stipulations in section 9.4.

9.4.5 Notice and Consent to Use Private Information

The CA may not provide any notice or obtain the consent of the subscriber in order to release private information in accordance with other stipulations of section 9.4.

9.4.6 Disclosure Pursuant to Judicial or Administrative Process

The CA shall not disclose private information to any third party unless authorized by this policy, required by law, government rule or regulation, or order of a court of competent jurisdiction.

9.4.7 Other Information Disclosure Circumstances

Instruction: If there are additional circumstances not already covered that might cause an organization operating a PKI to disclose sensitive or private information, it should be described here. Otherwise this section may be "Not Applicable" or "None."

9.5 Intellectual Property Rights

The CA shall not knowingly violate intellectual property rights held by others.

9.6 Representations and Warranties

9.6.1 CA Representations and Warranties

CAs operating under this policy shall warrant that their procedures are implemented in accordance with this CP, and that any certificates issued that assert the policy OIDs identified in this CP were issued in accordance with the stipulations of this policy.

A CA that issues certificates that assert a policy defined in this document shall conform to the stipulations of this document, including—

- Providing a CPS, as well as any subsequent changes, for conformance assessment.
- Maintaining its operations in conformance to the stipulations of the CPS.
- Ensuring that registration information is accepted only from approved RAs operating under an approved CPS.
- Including only valid and appropriate information in certificates, and maintaining evidence that due diligence was exercised in validating the information contained in the certificates.
- Revoking the certificates of subscribers found to have acted in a manner counter to their obligations in accordance with section 9.6.3.
- Operating or providing for the services of an on-line repository, and informing the repository service provider of their obligations if applicable.

9.6.2 RA Representations and Warranties

An RA that performs registration functions as described in this policy shall comply with the stipulations of this policy, and comply with a CPS approved by the Policy Authority for use with this policy. An RA who is found to have acted in a manner inconsistent with these obligations is subject to revocation of RA responsibilities. An RA supporting this policy shall conform to the stipulations of this document, including—

- Maintaining its operations in conformance to the stipulations of the approved CPS.
- Including only valid and appropriate information in certificate requests, and maintaining evidence that due diligence was exercised in validating the information contained in the certificate.
- Ensuring that obligations are imposed on subscribers in accordance with section 9.6.3, and that subscribers are informed of the consequences of not complying with those obligations.

9.6.3 Subscriber Representations and Warranties

A subscriber (or AOR for device certificates) shall be required to acknowledge acceptance of the requirements the subscriber shall meet respecting protection of the private key and use of the certificate before being issued the certificate.

Subscribers shall—

- Accurately represent themselves in all communications with the PKI authorities.
- Protect their private key(s) at all times, in accordance with this policy, as stipulated in their certificate acceptance agreements and local procedures.
- Promptly notify the appropriate CA upon suspicion of loss or compromise of their private key(s). Such notification shall be made directly or indirectly through mechanisms consistent with the CA's CPS.

- Abide by all the terms, conditions, and restrictions levied on the use of their private key(s) and certificate(s).

9.6.4 Relying Parties Representations and Warranties

Instruction: This CP does not specify the steps a relying party should take to determine whether to rely upon a certificate. The relying party decides, pursuant to its own policies, what steps to take. The CA merely provides the tools (i.e., certificates and CRLs) needed to perform the trust path creation, validation, and CP mappings that the relying party may wish to employ in its determination. Describe in this section any representations and warranties the CA is required to make to relying parties. If none are required, state 'Not Applicable'.

9.6.5 Representations and Warranties of Other Participants

Instruction: If a PKI implementation has additional participants not covered by the other subsections of 9.6 who nevertheless need to be held to particular behavioral standards (representations and warranties), they should be described here. Otherwise this section may be marked "Not Applicable" or "None".

9.7 Disclaimers of Warranties

CAs operating under this policy shall not disclaim any responsibilities described in this CP.

9.8 Limitations of Liability

Instruction: Organizations determining whether to "trust" a PKI will generally look at this section to determine the degree of responsibility a PKI is willing to take for its actions. Appropriate text for this section may include:

- *A statement that liability and the limitation thereof will be set forth in applicable agreements between the PKI/CA and its affiliates/customers/etc.*
- *A statement to the effect that the PKI/CA shall not be liable for any indirect damages of any kind, including consequential, incidental, special, punitive, or other damages whatsoever arising out of or related to the CP, even if advised of the possibility of such damages.*
- *A statement limiting liability to direct damages actually incurred as a result of improper actions by the CA or CA personnel and limited to <monetary amount> per incident (misuse relating to a failure on the part of the CA due to a particular occurrence of negligence, regardless of the number of relying parties (claimants) involved).*

9.9 Indemnities

Instruction: When organizations seek to establish trust relationships with external organizations, there may be need to establish indemnification clauses to protect the parties to the trust relationship. In some situations where there are contractual agreements, indemnity may be contained in the contractual language, otherwise it may be provided in this section.

9.10 Term and Termination

9.10.1 Term

Instruction: This section documents the term for which the CP is effective.

1   **9.10.2 Termination**

2   *Instruction: This section documents under what conditions the CP may be terminated.*

3   **9.10.3 Effect of Termination and Survival**

4   The requirements of this CP shall remain in effect through the end of the archive period for the last
5   certificate issued.

6   **9.11 Individual Notices and Communications with Participants**

7   The Policy Authority shall establish appropriate procedures for communications with CAs operating
8   under this policy via contracts or memoranda of agreement as applicable.

9   **9.12 Amendments**

10 **9.12.1 Procedure for Amendment**

11 The Policy Authority shall review this CP at least once every year. Corrections, updates, or changes to
12 this CP shall be publicly available. Suggested changes to this CP shall be communicated to the contact in
13 section 1.5.2; such communication must include a description of the change, a change justification, and
14 contact information for the person requesting the change.

15 **9.12.2 Notification Mechanism and Period**

16 Whenever the CP is amended, it shall be published within <30> days of the date the amendment took
17 place and all known concerned parties (OA staff, relying parties, subscribers, etc.) shall be notified.

18 *Instruction: The Policy Authority establishing the CP is encouraged to practice sound version*
19 *management, updating version numbers and effective dates appropriately to avoid confusion. Older*
20 *versions of the CP should be made available for reference and comparison.*

21 **9.12.3 Circumstances under which OID must be Changed**

22 *Instruction: Describe in this section whether this is required, and any other circumstances requiring OID*
23 *change. OIDs should be changed if there is a change in the CP that reduces the level of assurance*
24 *provided.*

25 **9.13 Dispute Resolution Provisions**

26 The Policy Authority shall facilitate the resolution between entities when conflicts arise as a result of the
27 use of certificates issued under this policy.

28 **9.14 Governing Law**

29 Subject to any limits appearing in applicable law, the laws of <the governing juridiction> shall govern the
30 enforceability, construction, interpretation, and validity of this CP, irrespective of contract or other choice
31 of law provisions.

32 **9.15 Compliance with Applicable Law**

33 All CAs operating under this policy shall comply with applicable law.

1 **9.16 Miscellaneous Provisions**

2 **9.16.1 Entire Agreement**

3 *Instruction: Any business or legal provisions pertaining to the PKI that have not been covered previously*
4 *in Section 9 should be identified here. Otherwise this may be "Not" Applicable or "None."*

5 **9.16.2 Assignment**

6 Except where specified by contract, no party may assign or delegate this CP or any of its rights or duties
7 under this CP, without the prior written consent of the other party (such consent not to be unreasonably
8 withheld), except that <PKI organization> may assign and delegate this CP to any party of its choosing.

9 **9.16.3 Severability**

10 Should it be determined that one section of this CP is incorrect or invalid, the other sections of this CP
11 shall remain in effect until the CP is updated. The process for updating this CP is described in section
12 9.12.

13 **9.16.4 Enforcement (Attorneys' Fees and Waiver of Rights)**

14 *Instruction: Organizations will include language here pertaining to the waiver of rights. For example:*
15 *"Any failure to exercise any right hereunder shall not be construed as a relinquishment of any future*
16 *exercise of such right."*

17 **9.16.5 Force Majeure**

18 *Instruction: Organizations will include language here specifying extreme conditions under which the PKI*
19 *will not be liable.*

20 **9.17 Other Provisions**

21 *Instruction: Any business or legal provisions pertaining to the PKI that have not been covered previously*
22 *in Section 9 should be identified here. Otherwise this may be "Not" Applicable or "None".*

Appendix A—Acronyms

Selected acronyms and abbreviations used in the guide are defined below.

AIA	Authority Information Access
AOR	Authorized Organizational Representative
CA	Certification Authority
COMSEC	Communications Security
CP	Certificate Policy
CPS	Certification Practice Statement
CRL	Certificate Revocation List
CSOR	Computer Security Objects Registry
CSR	Certificate Signing Request
CSS	Certificate Status Server
DN	Distinguished Name
ECDSA	Elliptic Curve Digital Signature Algorithm
FIPS PUB	(US) Federal Information Processing Standards Publication
FPKI	Federal Public Key Infrastructure
HTTP	Hypertext Transfer Protocol
IEC	International Electrotechnical Commission
IETF	Internet Engineering Task Force
IS	Information System
LAN	Local Area Network
LDAP	Lightweight Directory Access Protocol
ISO	International Organization for Standardization
ITU-T	International Telecommunications Union – Telecommunications Sector
NIST	National Institute of Standards and Technology
NSTISSI	National Security Telecommunications and Information Systems Security Instruction
OCSP	Online Certificate Status Protocol

OID	Object Identifier
OZ	Operations Zone
PIN	Personal Identification Number
PIV	Personal Identity Verification
PKCS	Public Key Cryptography Standards
PKI	Public Key Infrastructure
PKIX	Public Key Infrastructure X.509
PSS	Probabilistic Signature Scheme
PZ	Public Zone
RA	Registration Authority
RZ	Restricted Zone
RFC	Request For Comments
RSA	Rivest-Shamir-Adleman (encryption algorithm)
RSASSA	RSA Signature Scheme with Appendix
SHA	Secure Hash Algorithm
S/MIME	Secure/Multipurpose Internet Mail Extensions
SAZ	Special Access Zone
SP	Special Publication
SSP-REP	Shared Service Provider Repository Service Requirements
TAM	Trust Anchor Manager
UPS	Uninterrupted Power Supply
URL	Uniform Resource Locator
U.S.C.	United States Code
UUID	Universal Unique Identifier
VPN	Virtual Private Network
WAP	Wireless Access Point

Appendix B—Glossary

Access	Ability to make use of any information system (IS) resource. [NS4009]
Access Control	Process of granting access to information system resources only to authorized users, programs, processes, or other systems. [NS4009]
Accreditation	Formal declaration by a Designated Approving Authority that an Information System is approved to operate in a particular security mode using a prescribed set of safeguards at an acceptable level of risk. [NS4009]
Activation Data	Private data, other than keys, that are required to access cryptographic modules (i.e., unlock private keys for signing or decryption events).
Anonymous	Having an unknown name.
Applicant	The subscriber is sometimes also called an "applicant" after applying to a certification authority for a certificate, but before the certificate issuance procedure is completed. [ABADSG footnote 32]
Archive	Long-term, physically separate storage.
Attribute Authority	An entity, recognized as having the authority to verify the association of attributes to an identity.
Audit	Independent review and examination of records and activities to assess the adequacy of system controls, to ensure compliance with established policies and operational procedures, and to recommend necessary changes in controls, policies, or procedures. [NS4009]
Audit Data	Chronological record of system activities to enable the reconstruction and examination of the sequence of events and changes in an event. [NS4009, "audit trail"]
Authenticate	To confirm the identity of an entity when that identity is presented.
Authentication	Security measure designed to establish the validity of a transmission, message, or originator, or a means of verifying an individual's authorization to receive specific categories of information. [NS4009]
Authorized Organizational Representative (AOR)	A person (potentially among several) within an organization who is authorized to vouch for non-person identities. Any particular AOR is not permanently linked to any particular non-person identity; the CA must only ascertain that the AOR is legitimately associated with the organization, and that the AOR is identified as having authority for the identity in question.
Backup	Copy of files and programs made to facilitate recovery if necessary.

[NS4009]

Bastion Host	A special purpose computer on a network specifically designed and configured to withstand attacks.
Binding	Process of associating two related elements of information. [NS4009]
Biometric	A physical or behavioral characteristic of a human being.
Certificate	A digital representation of information which at least (1) identifies the certification authority issuing it, (2) names or identifies its subscriber, (3) contains the subscriber's public key, (4) identifies its operational period, and (5) is digitally signed by the certification authority issuing it. [ABADSG]. As used in this CP, the term "certificate" refers to X.509 certificates that expressly reference the OID of this CP in the certificatePolicies extension.
Certification Authority (CA)	An authority trusted by one or more users to issue and manage X.509 public key certificates and CRLs.
CA Facility	The collection of equipment, personnel, procedures and structures that are used by a certification authority to perform certificate issuance and revocation.
CA Operating Staff	CA components are operated and managed by individuals holding trusted, sensitive roles.
Certificate Policy (CP)	A certificate policy is a specialized form of administrative policy tuned to electronic transactions performed during certificate management. A certificate policy addresses all aspects associated with the generation, production, distribution, accounting, compromise recovery and administration of public key certificates. Indirectly, a certificate policy can also govern the transactions conducted using a communications system protected by a certificate-based security system. By controlling critical certificate extensions, such policies and associated enforcement technology can support provision of the security services required by particular applications.
Certification Practice Statement (CPS)	A statement of the practices that a CA employs in issuing, suspending, revoking, and renewing certificates and providing access to them, in accordance with specific requirements (i.e., requirements specified in this CP, or requirements specified in a contract for services).
CPS Summary	A publically releasable version of the CPS.
Certificate-Related Information	Information, such as a subscriber's postal address, that is not included in a certificate. May be used by a CA managing certificates.
Certificate Revocation List (CRL)	A list maintained by a certification authority of the certificates that it has issued that are revoked prior to their stated expiration date.

Certificate Status Server (CSS)	A trusted entity that provides on-line verification to a relying party of a subject certificate's revocation status, and may also provide additional attribute information for the subject certificate.
Client (application)	A system entity, usually a computer process acting on behalf of a human user that makes use of a service provided by a server.
Compromise	Disclosure of information to unauthorized persons, or a violation of the security policy of a system in which unauthorized intentional or unintentional disclosure, modification, destruction, or loss of an object may have occurred. [NS4009]
Computer Security Objects Registry (CSOR)	Computer Security Objects Registry operated by the National Institute of Standards and Technology.
Confidentiality	Assurance that information is not disclosed to unauthorized entities or processes. [NS4009]
Cross-Certificate	A certificate used to establish a trust relationship between two certification authorities.
Cryptographic Module	The set of hardware, software, firmware, or some combination thereof that implements cryptographic logic or processes, including cryptographic algorithms, and is contained within the cryptographic boundary of the module. [FIPS 140]
Data Integrity	Assurance that the data are unchanged from creation to reception.
Digital Signature	The result of a transformation of a message by means of a cryptographic system using keys such that a relying party can determine: (1) whether the transformation was created using the private key that corresponds to the public key in the signer's digital certificate; and (2) whether the message has been altered since the transformation was made.
End Entity Certificate	A certificate in which the subject is not a CA (also known as a subscriber certificate).
Firewall	Gateway that limits access between networks in accordance with local security policy. [NS4009]
Integrity	Protection against unauthorized modification or destruction of information. [NS4009]. A state in which information has remained unaltered from the point it was produced by a source, during transmission, storage, and eventual receipt by the destination.
Intellectual Property	Useful artistic, technical, and/or industrial information, knowledge or ideas that convey ownership and control of tangible or virtual usage and/or representation.
Intermediate CA	A CA that is subordinate to another CA, and has a CA subordinate to itself.

Key Escrow	A deposit of the private key of a subscriber and other pertinent information pursuant to an escrow agreement or similar contract binding upon the subscriber, the terms of which require one or more agents to hold the subscriber's private key for the benefit of the subscriber, an employer, or other party, upon provisions set forth in the agreement. [adapted from ABADSG, "Commercial key escrow service"]
Key Exchange	The process of exchanging public keys in order to establish secure communications.
Key Management Key	Key exchange, key agreement, key transport
Key Pair	Two mathematically related keys having the properties that (1) one (public) key can be used to encrypt a message that can only be decrypted using the other (private) key, and (2) even knowing the public key, it is computationally infeasible to discover the private key.
Key Rollover Certificate	The certificate that is created when a CA signs a new public key for itself with its old private key, and vice versa
Modification (of a certificate)	The act or process by which data items bound in an existing public key certificate, especially authorizations granted to the subject, are changed by issuing a new certificate.
Mutual Authentication	Occurs when parties at both ends of a communication activity authenticate each other (see authentication).
Non-Repudiation	Assurance that the sender is provided with proof of delivery and that the recipient is provided with proof of the sender's identity so that neither can later deny having processed the data. [NS4009] Technical non-repudiation refers to the assurance a relying party has that if a public key is used to validate a digital signature, that signature had to have been made by the corresponding private signature key.
Object Identifier (OID)	A specialized formatted number that is registered with an internationally recognized standards organization, the unique alphanumeric/numeric identifier registered under the ISO registration standard to reference a specific object or object class. In the Federal PKI, OIDS are used to uniquely identify certificate policies and cryptographic algorithms.
Online Certificate Status Protocol	Protocol which provides on-line status information for certificates.
Operations Zone (OZ)	Network area containing systems for routine business operations.
Out-of-Band	Communication between parties utilizing a means or method that differs from the current method of communication (e.g., one party uses U.S. Postal Service mail to communicate with another party where current communication is occurring on-line).

Policy Authority (PA)	Body established to oversee the creation and update of certificate policies, review certification practice statements, review the results of CA audits for policy compliance, evaluate non-domain policies for acceptance within the domain, and generally oversee and manage the PKI certificate policies.
Privacy	Restricting access to subscriber or relying party information in accordance with Federal law.
Private Key	(1) The key of a signature key pair used to create a digital signature. (2) The key of an encryption key pair that is used to decrypt confidential information. In both cases, this key must be kept secret.
Pseudonym	A subscriber name that has been chosen by the subscriber that is not verified as meaningful by identity proofing. [NS4009]
Public Key	(1) The key of a signature key pair used to validate a digital signature. (2) The key of an encryption key pair that is used to encrypt confidential information. In both cases, this key is normally made publicly available in the form of a digital certificate.
Public Key Infrastructure (PKI)	A set of policies, processes, server platforms, software, and workstations used for the purpose of administering certificates and public/private key pairs, including the ability to issue, maintain, and revoke public key certificates.
Public Zone (PZ)	Network area that is not behind a protective boundary controlled by the organization.
Registration Authority (RA)	An entity that is responsible for identification and authentication of certificate subjects, but that does not sign or issue certificates (i.e., a registration authority is delegated certain tasks on behalf of an authorized CA).
Re-key (a certificate)	To change the value of a cryptographic key that is being used in a cryptographic system application; this normally entails issuing a new certificate that contains the new public key.
Relying Party	A person or entity who has received information that includes a certificate and a digital signature verifiable with reference to a public key listed in the certificate, and is in a position to rely on them.
Renew (a certificate)	The act or process of extending the validity of the data binding asserted by a public key certificate by issuing a new certificate.
Repository	A database containing information and data relating to certificates as specified in this CP; may also be referred to as a directory.
Restricted Zone (RZ)	Controlled network area for sensitive data processing and storage
Revoke a Certificate	To prematurely end the operational period of a certificate effective at a

specific date and time.

Risk	An expectation of loss expressed as the probability that a particular threat will exploit a particular vulnerability with a particular harmful result.
Root CA	In a hierarchical PKI, the CA whose public key serves as the most trusted datum (i.e., the beginning of trust paths) for a security domain.
Security Auditor	An individual (e.g. employee, contractor, consultant, 3rd party) who is responsible for auditing the security of CAs or Registration Authorities (RAs), including reviewing, maintaining, and archiving audit logs; and performing or overseeing internal audits of CAs or RAs. A single individual may audit both CAs and RAs. Security Auditor is an internal role that is designated as trusted.
Server	A system entity that provides a service in response to requests from clients.
Signature Certificate	A public key certificate that contains a public key intended for verifying digital signatures rather than encrypting data or performing any other cryptographic functions.
Special Access Zone (SAZ)	Highly controlled network area for processing and storage of especially high value data.
Subordinate CA	In a hierarchical PKI, a CA whose certificate signature key is certified by another CA, and whose activities are constrained by that other CA. (See superior CA).
Subscriber	A subscriber is an entity that (1) is the subject named or identified in a certificate issued to that entity, (2) holds a private key that corresponds to the public key listed in the certificate, and (3) does not itself issue certificates to another party. This includes, but is not limited to, an individual, an application or network device.
Superior CA	In a hierarchical PKI, a CA that has certified the certificate signature key of another CA, and that constrains the activities of that CA. (See subordinate CA).
Threat	Any circumstance or event with the potential to cause harm to an information system in the form of destruction, disclosure, adverse modification of data, and/or denial of service. [NS4009]
Trust List	Collection of Trusted Certificates used by relying parties to authenticate other certificates.
Trust Zone	The level of security controls in a network segment.
Trusted Agent	Entity authorized to act as a representative of a CA in confirming subscriber identification during the registration process. Trusted agents do not have automated interfaces with certification authorities.

Trust Anchor Manager	Authorities who manage a repository of trusted Root CA Certificates. They act on behalf of relying parties, basing their decisions on which CAs to trust on the results of compliance audits. A TAM sets requirements for inclusion of a CA's root public key in their store. These requirements are based on both security and business needs. The TAM has a duty to enforce compliance with these requirements, for example, requirements around the supply of audit results, on initial acceptance of a root, and on an ongoing basis. TAMs will follow their normal practice of requiring CAs to submit an annual audit report.
Trusted Certificate	A certificate that is trusted by the relying party on the basis of secure and authenticated delivery. The public keys included in trusted certificates are used to start certification paths. Also known as a "trust anchor".
Two-Person Control	Continuous surveillance and control of positive control material at all times by a minimum of two authorized individuals, each capable of detecting incorrect and/or unauthorized procedures with respect to the task being performed and each familiar with established security and safety requirements. [NS4009]
Zeroize	A method of erasing electronically stored data by altering the contents of the data storage so as to prevent the recovery of the data. [FIPS 140]
Zone Boundary	The limit of authority over the security of the data processed within the boundary.

Appendix C—References

ABADSG	Digital Signature Guidelines, 1996-08-01. http://www.abanet.org/scitech/ec/isc/dsgfree.html
CABF Base	CA Browser Forum Baseline Requirements for the Issuance and Management of Publicly-Trusted Certificates, v.1.1, 14 Sep 2012. https://www.cabforum.org/Baseline_Requirements_V1_1.pdf
CABF EV	Guidelines for the Issuance and Management of Extended Validation Certificates, version 1.4, 29 May 2012. https://www.cabforum.org/Guidelines_v1_4.pdf
CCP-PROF	X.509 Certificate and Certificate Revocation List (CRL) Extensions Profile for the Shared Service Providers (SSP) Program. http://www.idmanagement.gov/fpkipa/documents/CertCRLprofileForCP.pdf
CIMC	Certificate Issuing and Management Components Family of Protection Profiles, version 1.0, October 31, 2001. http://csrc.nist.gov/pki/documents/CIMC_PP_20011031.pdf
E-Auth	E-Authentication Guidance for Federal Agencies, M-04-04, December 16, 2003. http://www.whitehouse.gov/omb/memoranda/fy04/m04-04.pdf
FIPS 140	Security Requirements for Cryptographic Modules, FIPS 140-2, May 25, 2001. http://csrc.nist.gov/publications/fips/fips140-2/fips1402.pdf
FIPS 186-4	Digital Signature Standard (DSS), FIPS 186-4, July 2013. http://nvlpubs.nist.gov/nistpubs/FIPS/NIST.FIPS.186-4.pdf
FOIACT	5 U.S.C. 552, Freedom of Information Act. http://www4.law.cornell.edu/uscode/5/552.html
ISO9594-8	ITU-T Recommendation X.509 (2005)	ISO/IEC 9594-8:2005, Information technology - Open Systems Interconnection - The Directory: Public-key and attribute certificate frameworks.
ITMRA	40 U.S.C. 1452, Information Technology Management Reform Act of 1996. http://www4.law.cornell.edu/uscode/40/1452.html
NAG69C	Information System Security Policy and Certification Practice Statement for Certification Authorities, rev C, November 1999.
NSD42	National Policy for the Security of National Security Telecom and Information Systems, 5 Jul 1990. http://snyside.sunnyside.com/cpsr/privacy/computer_security/nsd_42.txt (redacted version)
NS4005	NSTISSI 4005, Safeguarding COMSEC Facilities and Material, August 1997.
NS4009	NSTISSI 4009, National Information Systems Security Glossary, January 1999.

PACS	*Technical Implementation Guidance: Smart Card Enabled Physical Access Control Systems*, Version 2.2, The Government Smart Card Interagency Advisory Board's Physical Security Interagency Interoperability Working Group, July 30, 2004. http://www.idmanagement.gov/smartcard/information/TIG_SCEPACS_v2.2.pdf
PKCS#1	Jakob Jonsson and Burt Kaliski, Public-Key Cryptography Standards (PKCS) #1: RSA Cryptography Specifications Version 2.1, RFC 3447, February 2003. http://www.ietf.org/rfc/rfc3447.txt
PKCS#12	PKCS 12 v1.0: Personal Information Exchange Syntax-June 24, 1999. ftp://ftp.rsasecurity.com/pub/pkcs/pkcs-12/pkcs-12v1.pdf
RFC 2119	Bradner, S., "Key words for use in RFCs to Indicate Requirement Levels", BCP 14, RFC 2119, March 1997. http://www.ietf.org/rfc/rfc2119.txt
RFC 2560	X.509 Internet Public Key Infrastructure: Online Certificate Status Protocol – OCSP, Michael Myers, Rich Ankney, Ambarish Malpani, Slava Galperin, and Carlisle Adams, June 1999. http://www.ietf.org/rfc/rfc2560.txt
RFC 2822	Internet Message Format, Peter W. Resnick, April 2001. http://www.ietf.org/rfc/rfc2822.txt
RFC 3647	Certificate Policy and Certification Practices Framework, Chokhani and Ford, Sabett, Merrill, and Wu, November 2003. http://www.ietf.org/rfc/rfc3647.txt
RFC 4122	A Universally Unique IDentifier (UUID) URN Namespace, Paul J. Leach, Michael Mealling, and Rich Salz, July 2005. http://www.ietf.org/rfc/rfc4122.txt
RFC 5280	Internet X.509 Public Key Infrastructure Certificate and Certificate Revocation List (CRL) Profile, D. Cooper etal, May 2008, http://www.ietf.org/rfc/rfc5280.txt
SP 800-37	Guide for the Security Certification and Accreditation of Federal Information Systems, NIST Special Publication 800-37, May 2004. http://csrc.nist.gov/publications/nistpubs/800-37/SP800-37-final.pdf
SP 800-63-2	Electronic Authentication Guideline, NIST Special Publication 800-63-2, Aug 2013. http://nvlpubs.nist.gov/nistpubs/SpecialPublications/NIST.SP.800-63-2.pdf
SP 800-88	NIST Special Publication 800-88: Guidelines for Media Sanitization http://csrc.nist.gov/publications/nistpubs/800-88/NISTSP800-88_with-errata.pdf
SP 800-53	NIST Special Publication 800-53: Recommendation for Security Controls for Federal Information Systems and Organizations http://csrc.nist.gov/publications/nistpubs/800-53-Rev3/sp800-53-rev3-final_updated-errata_05-01-2010.pdf
SP 800-61	NIST Computer Security Incident Handling Guide, Rev 2. National Institute of Standards and Technology, http://csrc.nist.gov/publications/nistpubs/800-61rev2/

SP800-61rev2.pdf

SP 800-57	NIST Special Publication 800-57 Rev 3, Recommendation for Key Management stpubs/800-61/sp800-61-revised2_Aug-2012.pdfndards and Technology □http://csrc.nist.gov/publications/nistpubs/800-57/sp800-57_part1_rev3_general.pdf
SSP REP	Shared Service Provider Repository Service Requirements. Federal PKI Policy Authority Shared Service Provider Working Group, December 13, 2011. http://www.idmanagement.gov/fpkipa/documents/SSPrepositoryRqmts.doc
SP 800-147	NIST Special Publication 800-147, BIOS Protection Guidelines. April 2011. http://csrc.nist.gov/publications/nistpubs/800-147/NIST-SP800-147-April2011.pdf
SP 800-147B	NIST Special Publication 800-147b, BIOS Protection Guidelines for Servers (Draft). July 2012. http://csrc.nist.gov/publications/drafts/800-147b/draft-sp800-147b_july2012.pdf